Your W

Your Well-being

How to get a job you will be good at and enjoy

Birendra & Anika,
I hope this is helpful in
planning a better working life
Best regards,
Mike

MIKE SMITH

EARLY REVIEWS

"If you want high-falutin' prose or trenchantly delivered opinions, you shouldn't read Mike Smith's new book, Your Work, Your Well-Being. But if you want simple, good advice, written engagingly and without artifice, that might actually make a big difference to your career and, importantly, your life overall, then I strongly recommend that you read it. We all spend enough of our time "at" work, whether in the office, at home or on the road, that it is beyond foolish not to look for a career (where that is possible) that can make us happy.

Mike is a straightforward man – with a straightforward message. But in a world where curation of a social media profile is deemed essential, where mental health issues have become more than commonplace and where genuine happiness is often hard to detect, his thinking around career and self is both attractive and necessary.

Rob Hands, previously Executive Managing Editor, The Times and The Sunday Times, now Commercial Operations Manager, RPC (a law firm)

"A pragmatic journey that seamlessly highlights the interoperability of happiness, well-being and professional life, where Mike Smith highlights some key steps toward achieving understanding - perhaps the most important first principle.

There might be good reason in the saying "live in the present", that reason being that "the present" is also "the gift", and something to be valued, in his book Smith helps you to identify that special place."

Craig Thomson
CEO and Operational Excellence Leader

"Reading Mike Smith's book has made me stop and question what's important in my life right now and what I could change to be happier. Anyone trying to balance a busy career and home life should read this (at least once) and take action!"

Chris Raynor, Chief People Officer, Swissport

"This is a wonderful book that clearly and concisely addresses complex issues. It is a must read for anyone wanting to improve their well-being. The author manages to tackle issues in a light-hearted yet obviously researched way. This is backed by his years of experience with clients. The book provides helpful strategies and tools including powerful questions to consider. It is clear, thoughtful and intelligent. It has the potential to be career-altering and is extremely accessible. The researched theory and first-hand knowledge makes this book an essential read for anyone wanting to be both happier and more effective. I could not recommend this more highly."

Louisa Elder
Certified Coach & Psychotherapist

"Mike Smith offers readers a smorgasbord of things to consider when contemplating how to optimise happiness when transitioning between jobs. Through his personal approach sharing stories of both himself and some of the several hundred clients he's worked with who have confronted this issue first hand, Mike reminds us about the interrelated nature of the work we do and the happiness we feel. His practical tips and advice on how to approach career transitions effectively, whilst developing clarity of purpose and intent, provides the reader with a useful set of tools and healthier perspectives to navigate what can be a challenging period in life."

Ross Emerson
Executive Coach and Leadership Expert

Published by Goldcrest Books International Ltd
www.goldcrestbooks.com
publish@goldcrestbooks.com

ISBN: 978-1-913719-48-7

CONTENTS

INTRODUCTION

Who is this book for?

Perhaps you are asking yourself questions along these lines:

- Are you reconsidering your work-life balance and what is really important in your life?
- Are you worried that you might lose your job (or perhaps have just lost it) and you are not sure what sort of job you really want next?
- Do you feel that you are in the wrong job, but really don't know what the right job would be for you?
- Are you hoping to be happier in your working life, or looking for a stronger sense of purpose?
- Are you mid-career but you have never seriously thought about what you really want out of your working life?
- Are you not sure how to increase the chances of getting the job – and maybe the salary – you want in practical terms? (e.g. having a good CV, being well-prepared for interviews, using your personal network to help you, how to use LinkedIn).

- Are you coming up to deciding when you might retire and are not sure how you will spend your time in retirement?
- Are you perhaps considering a more radically different direction such as starting your own business?

If the answer to one or more of these questions is yes, then this book is for you.

Why did I write it and why should you read it?

First, I have written this book because I believe that the knowledge and insights I have gained from accompanying over three hundred individual clients on their transitions between jobs over the last twelve years are worth sharing.

Second, I have read many books about how to manage your career, and many about happiness and well-being, but I have seen very few that effectively combine what we know about well-being and how to manage your working life that are based both upon the experience of working with real people and the findings of substantial research.

This book, therefore, brings together the worlds of work and well-being in a way that I hope will be helpful to you. Putting modesty aside, my clients say fairly regularly that I have changed their lives for the better, and I hope that if you read this book, and importantly do the work and exercises I suggest you need to do, it will help you make positive changes in your life too. You could think of it as a guide to slow thinking about your future. I believe that slow thinking is like slow cooking – something we don't do enough of – and that if you do some of this higher-quality thinking at the beginning of your journey, you are much more likely to achieve your goals and do so more quickly.

Like many of the clients I have worked with over the last twelve years in career transition, you might be rather worried, or not very clear about your future. This book will help you become a lot clearer about which working future would be best for you, and then help you bring it about. It contains both evidence-based and practical (not just inspirational) advice as well as many workbook style exercises. Although it is written primarily from a UK context, about one third of my clients come from outside the UK – and I have spent about half my own working life outside the UK – so my outlook is essentially international. Most of the principles, e.g. learning from your past, being clear about your preferred future, the importance of networking, are all international in application.

It may surprise you to learn that research shows that improving your and your colleagues' level of well-being at work is also likely to:

- help you live a longer and healthier life
- help you be more productive
- help your organisation become more profitable and effective.

Improving the overall level of well-being could even potentially reduce the amount of tax we all have to pay because it would reduce health (or rather illness) and welfare costs.

This book suggests what you can do as an individual to improve your own level of well-being, but also considers (more briefly) the benefits of well-being for your organisation and to society as a whole.

In short, ***everybody wins if you are happier at work.***

If you are interested in learning more about well-being and how you can improve your own level of well-being, you might find it helpful to watch my TEDx talk:

www.youtube.com/watch?v=WMD02R0rMCc

How much choice do you have?

Some people in practical terms, and particularly in the short term, have very little choice about the type of work they do. Many will be urgently concerned about how to afford enough food or pay their energy and other bills. This is their very hard, day-to-day reality.

On the other hand, particularly over the medium to longer terms, many of us have more choice than we might at first think we do. One of the more powerful ideas in this book is that research (discussed in Chapter 1 in more detail) shows that only 10% of our level of well-being depends upon our upbringing, 50% is due to genetic factors, but the remaining 40% depends upon voluntary choices that we make: how we choose to spend our time, with whom and doing what. This is where we can exercise quite a lot of choice – particularly over the medium term – and so we can improve our level of well-being by consciously working at it.

I also present some real client cases of individuals, who successfully escaped from their very difficult pasts and succeeded in creating their own, much better futures.

I hope that many of you will find this knowledge liberating.

Beginning with you

Let's begin with you as an individual.

In living our lives, time is perhaps the most precious thing we have, deciding how we spend it, and with whom, will to quite a large degree, determine the overall quality of our lives and thus how happy we are. There are limitless ways we can spend our time, but we only have a limited amount of it, and the less we have the quicker it seems to pass. (Read Oliver Burkeman's excellent book: *Four Thousand Weeks*). For this reason, the choices we make about how to spend our time are critical. Ultimately, we have to account to ourselves for our decisions. To be able to make best use of our time we need to equip ourselves to make the best decisions possible, which take into account both a realistic understanding of ourselves and our insights into the world around us.

This is particularly important in that part of our lives in which most of us are likely to spend a great deal of our time: the world of our work. Finding out what type of work we will be best suited to, and which we will enjoy and be successful in, is one of the things that will most affect the overall quality of our lives.

One of my clients, in considering his future, used a phrase that I think expresses this well: "It is all about the quality of life remaining". In talking to a group of middle-aged clients, David Cooper pointed out that if your life as a whole is represented by one week, today is now Saturday afternoon for you– and so it is worthwhile thinking about how you would like the quality of your remaining life to be – and then working to make it that way.

What you should gain from reading this book

If you read this book, do the exercises in it thoughtfully and put real effort into your plan to find a more satisfying job you can expect to:

- have a clearer idea of who you are and what you do best.
- be much better prepared to find, and more likely to get, a job that you will both enjoy and do well.
- be happier in both your job and life as a whole.
- be less likely to have serious regrets in later life.

The main ideas it is based upon

The book is based upon five ideas that substantially flow from research:

- If you forget about your career, and manage your life, both will be better.
- We should focus on those things that we can actually influence or control and then deliberately nudge our lives in the direction in which we really want to go on a daily basis.

- Positive thoughts are not enough – we have to work at it to be happy.
- Regret in later life is one of the biggest risks to our long-term happiness – and one that would be irreversible – but we can plan now to avoid it later.
- If we improve our overall level of well-being, we are likely to live longer and healthier lives, and help our organisations be more effective and profitable.

The dangers of speed

One of the first clients I worked with had just been "let go" from a senior executive role in the USA. He was very action oriented and determined to get another job quickly. He wanted me to immediately help him write his CV and prepare him for interviews. Fortunately, he had been paid a decent amount on leaving his previous employer.

At our second discussion I said to him: "My main concern about you is that you are running so fast you are in danger of catching the wrong train" i.e. if he did not properly use the opportunity he had been given to really think about what he wanted to do next, he ran the risk of taking the first job offered, which he might be unhappy in and not good at and therefore risked being back on the job market after a short period, and hence becoming demotivated, less confident in his abilities and having a difficult story to tell about why he had only been in his most recent job for a short time.

We agreed that we should try and reduce that risk by thinking carefully about what he should do next. After a few months, he got a job he was very happy with and good at – having thought about it carefully and with some help from me.

Of course, many of us will be in a financial position where we don't have the choice of taking some time to think about what we really want to do but just have to start earning money again as quickly as possible, but if we are able to do so, it will be a good investment to think carefully about what sort of job will be best for us.

Hence, one of the most difficult and important things to do as a coach is sometimes to slow clients down – and thereby help them make high-quality decisions about their future.

Style and structure

David Cooper suggested the basic ideas behind the book, for which I am very thankful. He also developed the important Four Quadrant model that I summarise in Chapter 4.

In writing, I adopt whichever perspective – personal, historic or scientific – that seems most appropriate. I often begin each chapter with a short personal story (most of us enjoy stories), summarise the material from research and experience that I think will be helpful on this issue, and then usually suggest some exercises you can do that will make it particularly relevant to your own circumstances. I include real (mostly anonymous) client stories in boxes. If there are quite a lot of new ideas in the chapter, I introduce the chapter, go through the material and then summarise. If the chapter is quite short and straightforward, I don't introduce or summarise.

The chapters are written so that it should be reasonably easy for you to dip in and out of each one in a more or less modular fashion, so there is occasional repetition in the content. If you are not interested, e.g. on preparing for interviews in the public sector, just skip that part.

The basic structure of the book is the journey that my clients typically go on:

- Learning from their past, e.g. what has actually made them happy and unhappy, and understanding themselves well so they can prepare for their preferred working future more effectively.
- Considering any practical constraints, e.g. financial.
- After considering various options, deciding on what they most want to do in a way that they can explain clearly and succinctly to friends, colleagues or recruiters in one or two sentences.
- Equipping themselves with effective tools to achieve their goals, e.g. preparing an effective CV and LinkedIn profile, using personal networking systematically, understanding the power of your personal image, preparing for interviews.
- Pursuing their objective systematically and energetically, while responding to unforeseen opportunities.

- Celebrating the little victories along the way and bouncing back from inevitable setbacks.
- Achieving the job (or collection of roles) that they wanted to achieve.

Because there are two areas in career transition – the power of image and the use of LinkedIn – I am not very expert in, I asked two of my colleagues (Melissa Lund – the power of image, and Lincoln Coutts – the use of LinkedIn and other social media) to contribute a chapter each in their own areas of expertise, which they have kindly done.

I also address in some detail many of the issues you will need to consider if you wish to explore the possibility of starting your own business. Because this is a very different path to pursuing another job, I put it at the end of the book in Chapter 16.

Illustrations

Many people enjoy and learn from pictures as well as words and so I have included simple illustrations by Morgan Gleave to make some of the ideas clearer. Morgan has also created the character, Jo Pilgrim, on the journey towards his/her future, and we have added a cartoon to each chapter to include some visual content and help bring the material to life.

The process works!

Many years ago, when we were expecting our first child in the next twenty-four hours, my elder brother, sympathetically understanding how nervous I was, said: "Listen, Mike. You need to understand – the process works!"

Having developed this approach by working with three hundred very different clients, I hope that you will find that this process works too!

Most of the material and exercises in the book have been tried and refined in use with my clients over quite a long period.

On this journey, I often encourage my clients to look at their future through the lens of their well-being. What type of work is likely to make them happier, and being happier, probably do a better job? In thinking about possible flexible working options post-pandemic, I also think it is appropriate to look at your preferred working future from the perspective of maximising your well-being, which will also likely improve your contribution to your employer.

I do hope that you will enjoy the journey – it will not come again!

CHAPTER 1

Why Happiness Matters and What Actually Makes You Happy?

The man who grew olive trees

One of my clients, Marco, whose story well illustrates several of the principles of what makes people happy, was responsible for managing the supply chain for a large Italian domestic appliance manufacturer. The company was being prepared for sale and so was intent on cutting costs to improve short-term apparent profitability. The company made my client redundant. Not surprisingly, his first reaction was to be very angry. ("I will show them that they made a huge mistake – by getting an amazing and well-paid job.") He tried to do this for a while, but while working with me, began to realise that he had just been paid quite a large amount as a redundancy payment and so, from a financial point of view, did not need to find a job immediately. He had the opportunity to think carefully about what he really wanted to do.

Marco and his olive trees

One of the things he remembered was that for some reason (I never did quite understand why) he had always wanted to grow olive trees. He therefore bought a relatively small parcel of land, on which olive trees had been grown using very traditional methods, and then planted many more. After a few years of hard work, he found he could earn about €100,000 p.a. from the olive oil produced from his land.

He had also always had an interest in property. As Italy was at the time in the depths of an economic crisis, property prices were particularly low and so he bought up some local properties for renovation with a view to either sale or rental.

Thirdly, he used his particular area of expertise (developing an efficient supply chain) by working as a consultant to smaller companies in the region, helping them on supply chain issues.

He could work with his son in the olive oil plantation, and if he wanted to take a holiday, he could easily go skiing for several weeks.

By doing these quite different things he found that he was now making more money that he had been in his last corporate role. More importantly, he was a great deal happier.

Marco made more substantial changes in his working life than many of us might consider, but his story illustrates very well how many of us can, if we really want to, reshape our lives and our working lives in a way that is likely to make us happier.

If we now consider his experience from a well-being point of view, his new life clearly demonstrates several of the principles we can deduce from the research discussed in more detail below:

1. He had a strong sense of ***P**urpose* – he had always wanted to grow olive trees.
2. He was able to invest in ***R**elationships* – he worked with his son on the olive plantation and got to know local property tradesmen well through his property business.
3. He was substantially in *Control* of his life – he had no boss and could largely choose which activity he wanted to pursue. By having three quite different income streams, he developed a relatively low risk portfolio – if he was very busy with one activity, he could usually scale down one or two of the others.
4. He was able to live in the ***P**resent* – having dealt with any regrets about the past and not being too anxious about his future.

5. He was able to take a good amount of *Exercise*, not only through the physical work of producing olive oil, but he could also go skiing at times of his choosing.

If it helps you remember this, you can think of these as being the ***PRinCiPlEs*** of happiness.

But what do we actually know about work and well-being from research?

Each of us is unique, with our individual experiences and motivations, but we do know a great deal about what works for most people in terms of helping them to be happy and effective in what they do. And the evidence is well worth considering seriously – in order to help us make better decisions about our preferred working future.

This chapter

In this chapter we will learn:

- Why happiness is important, both to you as an individual and to your organisation. You may well learn from the research that it is quite a lot more important than you might have guessed.
- About Martin Seligman's Happiness Formula, which states that you *can* influence or control some 40% of how happy you are likely to be by choosing what sort of activities, in what sort of place and with whom you will mainly prefer to spend your time.

- What you can do to make yourself happier – five things that should increase your medium- and long-term level of well-being.
- That more money alone, once you have enough to place a roof over your head and can look after your family's basic needs (if you have one), may not be enough to make you happier.
- You will have to work hard to become happier – it is very unlikely to happen just because you would like it to.
- Organisations where employees are more engaged (and are therefore likely to be happier) are more profitable than where they are not.

Why does happiness matter in the first place?

Individuals

In one of my favourite research projects in positive psychology (largely the study of what makes people well, rather than the study of what makes people ill) a community of nuns was studied. (Danner, Snowdon and Friesen, 2001). *Note: in my choice of research, I like to look at both old and newer research – we sometimes learnt important things a long time ago.*

Nuns were chosen because they have less variety in their lives than many of us – they live in the same place, eat the same food and have a structured and similar day to day existence – so there are less variables in their lives than is the case for most of us.

Three sisters visit Cherai Beach in Kerala, India.
Photo by Michael Foley, Dublin

When each of the nuns had joined the community, they had been asked to write a personal statement of why they were doing so. The experiment simply consisted of analysing how positive or negative the language of each of their individual personal statements was and then following their health histories for many years afterwards.

The results were quite astounding – ***the nuns with the most positive personal statements, lived on average, a decade longer than their more negative colleagues***, and intriguingly, had a lower level of Alzheimer's disease.

In a striking and updated version of similar research (Eichstaedt, et. al. 2015) the language of Twitter feeds was analysed in a part of the USA in terms of how positive or negative the language was in a particular geographic area.

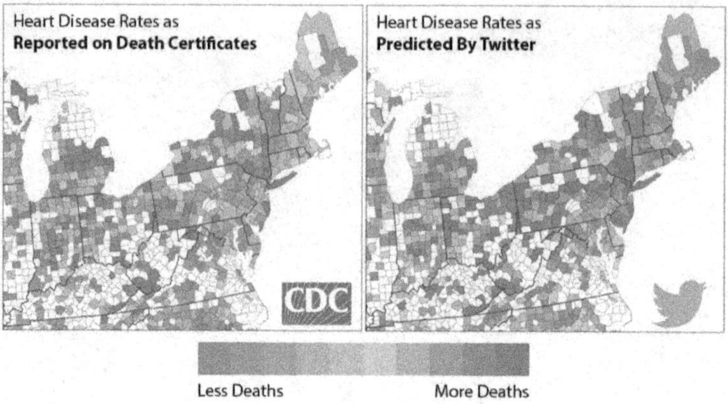

University of Pennsylvania 2015

The results showed that the more negative the language used on Twitter in a given area, the higher the likelihood was of death from cardiovascular disease. In the local communities there was a higher correlation between negative or angry language on Twitter and death from heart disease than for any other more conventional factors such as poverty or obesity.

Internet trolls should consider this research quite seriously! It could be that they will die rather earlier than their happier neighbours if they persist in being so angry in their language.

Also, in another study, Martin Seligman[1] (2008) found that once someone had had a first heart attack, the best way of predicting whether they would have a second was to assess how optimistic or pessimistic they were. Eight and a half years after their first heart attack, of the sixteen most pessimistic men in the study, fifteen had died; of the sixteen most optimistic men, only five had died.

---

1. American psychologist and author of several self-help books

If you are relatively happy, you are therefore likely to live approximately a decade longer – and other research shows, you will also be likely to live a relatively healthier life.

Happier individuals also:

- get promoted faster
- earn more
- get more support
- generate better and more creative ideas
- achieve goals faster
- interact better with colleagues and bosses
- receive superior reviews
- learn more
- achieve greater success
- are healthier.[2]

The happiness formula – and your childhood is not your fate

Everybody wins when we are happier.

Can we change our personal level of well-being? What do we know from research about how much we can influence or control our level of happiness?

Martin Seligman developed a formula for happiness. Research suggests that roughly 50% of our general

2. *List courtesy of executive coach Jessica Pryce-Jones, 2010*

level of happiness turns out to be attributable to our genetic inheritance. It is equally interesting that very little (10%) depends upon the actual circumstances of your childhood – so you should not keep blaming the circumstances of your early childhood for your life now, or your future life. Hence, you are in more control of your happiness than you might think:

> *I think that the events of childhood are overrated; in fact, I think that past history in general is overrated. It has turned out to be difficult to find even small effects of childhood events on adult personality, and there is no evidence at all of large – to say nothing of determining – effects.*
>
> *The major traumas of childhood may have some influence on adult personality but only a barely detectable one. Bad childhood events, in short, do not mandate adult troubles. There is no justification in these studies for blaming your adult depression, anxiety, bad marriage, drug use, sexual problems, unemployment, aggression against your children, alcoholism, or anger on what happened to you as a child.*

Seligman, 2008

This view was strongly reinforced by the recent and authoritative conclusions from Robert Waldinger's and Mark Schulz's book *The Good Life and How to Live it – Lessons from the World's Longest Study on Happiness.* Their book is based upon The Harvard Study of Adult Development, which began in 1938 and has continued to include three generations and more than 1,300 of the descendants of the original 724 participants. One of their important conclusions is:

> "Your childhood is not your fate. Your natural disposition is not your fate. The neighbourhood you grew up in is not your fate. The research shows this clearly. Nothing that has happened in your life precludes you from connecting with others, from thriving, or from being happy. People often think that once you get to adulthood, that's it – your life and your way of living are set. But what we find by looking at the entirety of research into adult development is that this just isn't true. Meaningful change is possible."

This is a very liberating idea; by the choices you make, you can substantially free yourself from what you might have felt were the chains of an unfortunate childhood.

Seligman's formula that represents happiness is as follows:

$$H = S + C + V$$

Where H is your enduring level of happiness, S is your set range, C are the circumstances of your life, and V represents factors under your voluntary control.

According to Sonja Lyubomirsky[3], a large portion (50% – see diagram on page 28) of what makes us happy is our genetic set point – what we have inherited – whilst the circumstances of our upbringing objectively have very little (10%) bearing on our happiness. The good news, therefore, is that quite a lot (40%) of how happy you are – the voluntary choices you make – *is* under your control; who you choose to be with, and doing what, will be very likely to have a substantial effect on your medium to long term level of happiness.

3. *Professor of Psychology and author of 'The How of Happiness'*

What you can do to make yourself happier

The habits of happy people

If you want to be happier, one thing you can do is imitate the habits of happy people.

Sonja Lyubomirsky points out that happy people tend to have quite a lot in common:

- They devote a great amount of time to their family and friends, nurturing and enjoying those relationships.
- They are comfortable expressing gratitude for all they have.
- They are often the first to offer helping hands to co-workers and passers-by.
- They practise optimism when imagining their future.
- They savour life's pleasures and try to live in the present moment.

- They make physical exercise a weekly, and even daily, habit.
- They are deeply committed to lifelong goals and ambitions, e.g. fighting fraud, building cabinets, or teaching their children their deeply held values.
- Last, but not least, the happiest people do have their share of stresses, crises and even tragedies. They may become just as distressed and emotional in such circumstances as you or me, but their secret weapon is the poise and strength they show in coping in the face of challenge.

If you consciously try to adopt more of the habits of happier people, you are likely to become happier in practice – you can "Fake it until you make it".

Notice that many of the habits of happy people, e.g. optimism, can apply both to a work and a social context.

Five things that should improve your level of well-being

What else can you actually do to improve your overall level of happiness or well-being?

From a substantial and evidence-based study in 2008, a UK Government report identified the well-being equivalent of five fruit and vegetables a day. Although the findings sound perhaps like things your mother might have said to you – and she would have been right – the suggestions for individual action, which are based on an extensive review of the actual research evidence, are:

- **Connect** –with the people around you. With family, friends, colleagues and neighbours. At home, work, school or in your local community. Think of these as the cornerstones of your life and invest time in developing them. Building these connections will support and enrich you every day.

- **Be active** – go for a walk or a run. Step outside; cycle; play a game; do some gardening; dance. Exercising makes you feel good. Most importantly, discover a physical activity you enjoy and that suits your level of mobility and fitness.

- **Take notice** – be curious. Catch sight of the beautiful. Remark on the unusual. Notice the changing seasons. Savour the moment, whether you are walking to work, eating lunch or talking to friends. Be aware of the world around you and what you are feeling. Reflecting on your experiences will help you appreciate what matters to you.

- **Keep learning** – try something new. Rediscover an old interest. Sign up for that course. Take on a different responsibility at work. Fix a bike. Learn to play an instrument or how to cook your favourite food. Set a challenge you enjoy achieving. Learning new things will make you more confident as well as being fun.

- **Give** – do something nice for a friend, or a stranger. Thank someone. Smile. Volunteer your time. Join a community group. Look out, as well as in. Seeing yourself, and your happiness, as linked to the wider community can be incredibly rewarding and creates connections with the people around you.

You can choose one of these to work on – and start immediately – try it today or tomorrow. If you enjoy it, you will be encouraged to do more.

Exercise and meditation

Whether in the work context or not, a great deal of the literature suggests that regular exercise is beneficial to improving higher levels of well-being (including the UK Government report above).

> *Aerobic exercise was just as effective at treating depression as was Zoloft (an anti-depressant drug), or as a combination of exercise and Zoloft...*
>
> *...Physical activity reduces anxiety and stress; protects us from dying in general (and from dying of heart disease or cancer in particular); reduces the risk of numerous diseases (diabetes, colon cancer, hypertension); builds bones, muscles, and joints; increases quality of life; improves sleep, protects against cognitive impairments as we age; and helps control weight. In sedentary older adults, a very low intensity exercise programme (walking or resistance training) reduces depression and increases confidence and maintains the improvement for an astonishing five years. Finally, surveys show, and large-scale interventions confirm, that exercise may very well be the most effective instant happiness booster of all activities.*
>
> **Lyubomirsky, 2008**

One of the more intriguing aspects of this is the beneficial effect of any form of exercise that produces a physiological effect called the relaxation response. Forms of exercise that produce this, such as yoga, meditation or t'ai chi, actually changes your DNA for the better. A Harvard University study, first published in 2008, found the first compelling evidence that the Relaxation Response (RR) – the physiological response to exercises such as meditation, yoga, t'ai chi, quigong or repetitive prayer – affects our genes. In other words, meditation – short or long term – causes hundreds of genes to turn on or off beneficially.

Many of the genes are involved in cellular metabolism and in the body's response to oxidative stress. Oxidative stress is one of the biological products of mental and emotional stress. It produces free radicals and is known to be involved in a host of disease processes, including atherosclerosis, Parkinson's disease and Alzheimer's disease. It also accelerates ageing at the cellular level. The scientists proposed that the relaxation response – whether it is induced through meditation, yoga or prayer – may counteract cellular damage due to chronic psychological stress.

My son, who had returned from doing voluntary work in Bangladesh a few years ago, was diagnosed with a quite severe case of Irritable Bowel Syndrome, which meant he was unable to eat a wide range of foods he enjoyed and had ongoing problems with his digestive system. A couple of years ago, he began to use a popular meditation app regularly. Within the last few months, nearly all of his symptoms have disappeared, and he is convinced this is because of his habit of meditation. One of the factors thought to make IBS more likely is ongoing stress.

People have meditated for years and enjoyed better health – and a slower ageing process – but many others have been sceptical as to its benefits. Now, we have solid scientific proof of the positive genetic effects of meditation in that it affects genes that positively influence cell metabolism and the response to oxidative stress.

Living in the present

About half the people I saw as I (used to!) commute in London are looking at their smart phones and not at the people or environment around them. Many managers will take their computers on holiday and check and respond to their emails – even though they are on holiday. Technology can now make you always available, which actually means that you are rarely living in the present, here and now.

> *A beautiful statue was erected in the grounds of Salisbury cathedral in the form of an arch over a well-trodden path. Not very long after it had been erected it was decided to take it down because too many people walking along the path had bumped their heads into the statue – few of them were enjoying their beautiful environment but were in the other world of their smart phones.*
>
> **Salisbury Journal, 18 February 2016**

It is increasingly recognised that practices that enable you to focus on your present situation, such as mindfulness training, meditation or yoga, help you to both relax and focus.

By living in the present, Lyubomirsky means that we try increasingly to:

- be non-judgemental
- be non-striving
- be patient
- be trusting
- be open
- let go.[4]

I am a personal fan and regular practitioner of yoga. From a large, if self-selected sample, the Yoga Biomedical Trust found that regular practise of yoga, according to those who practised it, found that it helped with a very wide range of ailments.

Conditions improved by yoga, self-reported

Condition	No. of people reporting	% helped
Anxiety	838	94
Arthritis	838	90
Back disorders	1,142	98
High blood pressure	150	84
Insomnia	542	82
Migraine	464	80
The Yoga Biomedical Trust, London, Survey of 2,700 who used yoga therapeutically, 1983–4		

4. *Lyubomirsky, 2008*

My own (diastolic) blood pressure came down by eight points after I started practising yoga regularly.

Achieving Flow

Another way in which you can improve your level of well-being is to look out for experiences that give you the feeling of Flow in your day-to-day life. This idea was developed by a Hungarian psychologist, Mihaly Csikszentmihalyi. Flow activities are those that are skilful, all absorbing and require a high level of personal engagement.

The particular attributes of Flow activities are:

- clear goals
- continuous and unambiguous feedback about progress
- opportunities that fully use personal capacity.

And you will know you're in Flow because you feel:

- intense concentration and focus
- a loss of self-consciousness
- distorted sense of time
- that your activity is rewarding in and of itself.

This sense of flow might be felt by a footballer, a musician, a businessman negotiating a complex deal, or you when you are exercising your favourite skill, or me when I am editing this book.

In thinking about your future working life – or how you might spend your spare time – you should think about, and seek out, opportunities that give you this sense of Flow. Even if you are in a role currently, you might seek out more opportunities to experience Flow activities through the choice of particular aspects of your job that use a high level of skills or experience, and which you enjoy.

Finding Flow: the man who made furniture

One of my clients, who had held a variety of senior jobs in his corporate life, came to our second meeting and said: "Mike, I have decided I don't want to do this anymore." (i.e. carry on in doing similar things to what he had been doing in a large corporation.)

I said that was fine.

"Do you know what you do want to do?"

"Yes," he said, "I want to make furniture."

We talked about what sort of business it could be, who his customers might be, what sort of products he could make and why did he think he could make money doing that.

I wanted to satisfy myself that this dramatic change in direction would actually make sense for him, that it would have a good chance of working out well and was not just a crazy pipe dream. I then remembered that when he told me the story of his career to date at our first meeting, he had mentioned that as a boy he had always enjoyed being around the engineering workshop that his dad had managed. The penny dropped for me when I had remembered reading about Flow – making chairs clearly gave him a strong sense of Flow: it was an activity that needed a high degree of skill and concentration and in which he immersed himself. He came to our third meeting with a photograph of a chair that he had made with a smile on his face.

"You see, I can do it!"

When he had made a chair, he sat in it and it either collapsed, or it didn't, and the customer smiled, or they did not – he received very clear and immediate feedback.

This was very different from his corporate life, where he had been responsible for very long, very complicated projects. Often, it was not clear whether they had been successful or not as many people had forgotten why they really started in the first place. If they were felt to have been successful, his boss, or others, had tended to take the credit. If they were felt to have not been very successful – perhaps because circumstances had changed as the project continued – he was made to feel responsible for their perceived failure, even if the change in circumstances was completely beyond his control. He was basically not in control of his working life.

In making furniture my client had found a Flow activity that worked for him. I bought some of the first furniture he made, which sits proudly in my back garden more than ten years later.

Managing time

Oliver Burkeman's book, *Four Thousand Weeks: Time and How to Use It, (2021),* challenges many of our habitual ways of thinking about our use of time. It is based upon the idea that, assuming you live to be eighty, you'll have had about four thousand weeks in your life.

Some of his helpful ideas are:

- It turns out that when people make enough money to meet their needs they just find new things to need and new lifestyles to aspire to. As a result, they work harder and harder, and soon busyness becomes an emblem of prestige, which is clearly completely absurd: for almost the whole of history, the entire point of being rich was *not* having to work so much.

- Denying reality never works, though. It may provide some immediate relief, because it allows you to go on thinking that at some point in the future you might, at last, feel totally in control. but it can't ever bring the sense you are doing enough – that you *are* enough – because it defines 'enough' as a kind of limitless control that no human can ever attain. Instead, the endless struggle leads to more anxiety and a less fulfilling life. For example, the more you believe you might succeed in 'fitting everything in', the more commitments you naturally take on, and the less you need to ask whether each new commitment is truly worth a portion of your time – and so your days inevitably fill up with activities you don't especially value.

- Our obsession with extracting the greatest future value out of our time blinds us to the reality that, in fact, the moment of truth is always now – that life is nothing but a succession of present moments, culminating in death, and that you'll probably never get to a point where you feel you have things in perfect working order. And that therefore you had better stop postponing the 'real meaning' of your existence into the future and throw yourself into life now.

It is therefore worth thinking carefully about our attitude to time and acknowledging that it is part of our human condition that we will never get everything done and that we should more usefully think about whether what we are doing in our series of present moments is of the most value to us and not, as the American novelist and essayist, Marilynne Robinson puts it, mere "Joyless urgency".

Having a sense of purpose

If you can find work with an organisation that has a sense of purpose you can identify with, you are more likely to be happy. Perhaps your employer is genuinely concerned about an important environmental problem, perhaps it is making a change for the better in people's lives, perhaps you agree with its political stance.

Professor Paul Dolan[5] believes that happiness is to be attained by alternately finding both pleasure and purpose in your everyday life.

---

5. Behavioural scientist and author

According to Jessica Pryce–Jones: "If you appreciate the values of your workplace, we've found you'll be happier, help your colleagues more, have higher trust and pride in your organisation, and intend to stay longer in your role."

For this to work for you over a long period the values expressed by the organisation have to be real and reflected in the actual behaviour of individuals who work there. In working with my clients, I have quite often come across organisations who make impressive statements in their annual reports about what their values are, but from my work with clients who actually worked there over a long period, it sometimes becomes obvious that the actual behaviour of people working there differed significantly from the organisation's formal statements. For example, in one leading financial services company that made impressive statements about their values, I worked with one client who had successfully brought a case of racial discrimination against them and another, from the same organisation, who had been the victim of bullying by his boss for many years and who, as a consequence, was seeing a psychiatrist and a psychologist at the time I was working with him. With help and support, he ended up taking a senior role in a large international bank.

In another example, I worked with six or seven clients who had worked for a large tobacco company for many years. Although the company was impressive in many other ways, all of these clients, without exception, did not want to continue working in the tobacco industry. They no longer wanted to associate themselves with their employer's basic purpose of growing and selling tobacco.

In thinking about your future role and organisation, you might therefore like to think, and gather what evidence is available (e.g., from past employees you might find via LinkedIn or from www.glassdoor.co.uk) about what it is really like to work for this organisation and whether it has an overall purpose that you can personally relate to. If, in reality, its sense of purpose or its actual values are not ones that you can personally support, you are unlikely to be happy and effective there. The stronger your personal values are, the more important it is to consider if the organisation's values are compatible with yours.

Feeling largely in control

Personal control is a much better predictor of happiness than income is.
Nettle, 2005

If you are working as a senior manager with responsibility for achieving a certain level of profits in a large organisation, it would not be unusual for your boss to say something like: "Mike, you just have to make these numbers, and we both know the alternative," while your team might say: "That is all very interesting boss, but you should understand that is never going to happen because it is impossible."

In a situation like this you are in a position where you have very little control – you are the meat in the sandwich and you are likely to have a low level of well-being. You are closer to feeling a victim of life than being a "master of the universe".

Feelings of low control have been shown to be connected to lethargy, burnout, time off sick, conflict at home, and, amazingly, heart disease too.
Pryce-Jones, 2010

Research by the American social psychologist and author, Jonathan Haidt, supports this view:

> 'In 1964, the sociologists Melvin Kohn and Carmi Schooler surveyed 3,100 American men about their jobs and found that the key to understanding which jobs were satisfying was what they called "occupational self-direction". Men who were closely supervised in jobs of low complexity and much routine showed the highest degree of alienation (feeling powerless, dissatisfied and separated from the work). Men who had more latitude in deciding how they approached work that was varied and challenging tended to enjoy their work much more.'

One of the challenges here is to clearly differentiate between what is within your control and what is not. It is no use to you at all to worry about issues such as the state of the economy or the general level of unemployment (although it will be useful to be *aware* of them) because you are unlikely to be able to exercise any degree of control over such large issues.

I personally like the quotation, usually attributed to the German philosopher Reinhold Niebuhr and known as the Serenity Prayer:

> *God, grant me the serenity to accept the things I cannot change, the courage to change the things I can, and the wisdom to know the difference.*

Investing in relationships

(Wo)Man is basically a social animal and an important part of evolutionary learning is that we do better collectively when we cooperate.

Whether it is in a work context or more broadly that of your family or community, you will be happier if you feel you have a strong network of constructive relationships around you.

Waldinger's and Schulz's *The Good Life* provides compelling evidence on this:

> 'When you're lonely, it hurts. And we don't mean that metaphorically. It has a physical effect on the body. Loneliness is associated with being more sensitive to pain, suppression of the immune system, diminished brain function, and less effective sleep, making an already lonely person even more tired and irritable. Recent research has shown that for older people loneliness is twice as unhealthy as obesity, and chronic loneliness increases a person's chance of death in any given year by 26 per cent.
>
> In the United States, in 2020, it was estimated that 162,000 deaths could be attributed to causes stemming from social isolation.'

Waldinger and Schulz found that what is really important to living a long and happy life are good, strong, warm relationships.

Loneliness kills and strong relationships are good for both your mind and body – so it is not about how many friends you have on Facebook but whether you have a network of people you care about and who care about you and who you can turn to when times get hard.

If your organisation is one where relationships are considered to be purely transactional (What have you done for me today?) or where employees are encouraged to compete with each other (e.g. in investment banking – peer competition for year-end bonuses) it is less likely to have highly engaged employees. As a result of this transactional approach, you are less likely to be happy in the work you are doing and therefore to live a long and healthy life.

Overcoming adversity: What does not kill you may make you stronger

Nearly everyone experiences events or circumstances in their lives that are difficult or distressing for them – and happy people suffer as much adversity as anyone else. Overcoming or coping with adversity is one of the things that may give you a better appreciation of the more truly valuable things in your life such as good health, or enjoyable times with your friends and family. (This is one lesson many of us have learnt or been reminded of living through the COVID19 Pandemic.)

Jonathan Haidt points out that research shows that although traumas, crises and tragedies come in a thousand forms, people benefit from them in three ways:

- Rising to a challenge reveals your hidden abilities, and seeing these abilities changes your self-concept. People are much stronger than they realised.

- Adversity is a filter. When a person is diagnosed with cancer, or a couple loses a child, some friends and family rise to the occasion and look for any way they can to express support or be helpful. One of the most common effects of losing a loved one was that the bereaved had a greater appreciation of and tolerance for the other people in his or her life.
- This change in ways of relating points to the third common benefit: Trauma changes priorities and philosophies towards the present (Live each day to the fullest) and towards other people.[6]

A client's story: overcoming adversity

In the first discussion with one of my clients I learnt that in the previous twelve months or so he:

- had been diagnosed with cancer
- was experiencing a difficult divorce
- had recently been fired by his former colleagues.

Not surprisingly, he was not sleeping well or taking regular exercise, and after I made it clear I am not a trained psychologist, I strongly encouraged him to seek medical help, which he did.

Over the next few months, we considered carefully:

- What had been the high points and achievements of his career to date.
- That research (Seligman, page 25) suggested that whatever negative challenges life had thrown at him

6. Haidt, 2006.

so far, he could very likely control about 40% of his own future level of well-being by choosing what sort of people he spent his time with, doing what.

- What exactly he ideally wanted to do in work terms (supported by the evidence from his past) and then developing and executing a plan to help him achieve his goal.

He was then able to talk very clearly with friends, colleagues and recruiters about what he wanted to do and why he wanted to do it, and he substantially achieved his goal – and in the process discovered that he was more in control of his life than he previously thought was possible. He managed to largely put his horrible experiences behind him, if not forget them.

A client who broke free from his upbringing

One of my private clients had a very tough upbringing. His dad used to beat his mum up and eventually hung himself in prison. My client was later convicted of manslaughter after defending a woman who was about to be raped at a party. He had killed the potential rapist in the knife fight that ensued. He subsequently served an eight-year prison sentence for manslaughter. He became a model prisoner.

He worked in the security industry and was heavily involved in a world of drugs, alcohol and violence. After his first child was born, however, he became determined to try and provide a better future for her than he had experienced in his own childhood and he managed to get a job in a service company, where he worked his way up to a managerial position.

I was introduced to him as a potential coaching client by the Human Resources director (a friend of mine) when he was on the point of being fired, mainly due to the poor relationships he had with several of his colleagues. His enlightened boss wanted to give him a chance of recovering his position provided his behaviour towards his colleagues changed for the better.

We had an initial discussion. My thinking was that as he had shown himself capable of pulling himself away from his previous world of violence, he may well be capable of making further improvements, and so should have another chance.

We began to work together. I interviewed his colleagues and fed back a summary of their views about my client to him. I asked my client what he wanted to obtain from our working together and he said he wanted to be respected as a manager. I suggested that was fine and I might be able to help him achieve his objective, but if he wanted to be respected, he would first of all have to respect himself and also be respectful of his colleagues, and only then might they be more respectful of him.

More importantly, I pointed out that research showed that in terms of an individual's level of well-being, about 50% was down to genetics – so nothing could be done there. Crucially, only 10% of his future level of well-being was likely due to his upbringing, however bad it had been. The remaining 40% would be due to the future choices he made. So, if he wanted to be respected as a manager, this could well happen if he made some choices in an appropriate direction (e.g. by being more respectful towards his colleagues). I would support him in making these changes.

We worked together over the next few months. One of his ideas was to see if he could develop an apprenticeship programme for ex-offenders who would then work in his company. I told him I thought this was a great idea and encouraged him to explore it. Eventually, he made a proposal to the company's board and gained their support.

After a few months, I conducted another survey of his colleagues and found that the changes that he had been making had been recognised by them and he was now a respected colleague. I fed back the summary of their changed views.

We soon agreed that it was an appropriate time to, using his words, "Cut the apron strings" and so my coaching support came to an end. In the words he used, he was, "A changed man."

I include this example as I think it a very clear case of how an individual, with support, can break free of a very difficult upbringing and successfully create their own better future, thus illustrating that 40% of our future level of well-being depends on the choices we make.

Money is unlikely to be enough to make you happy

There has been a great deal of research done on the relationship between money and happiness. The consensus view is that above a quite low level, an increase in income is unlikely, of itself, to bring about a corresponding degree of increase in well-being.

> 'Data from the Gallup World Poll, (a survey of happiness in 132 countries around the world) show that richer people in any country do not always feel

> happier than poorer ones. And beyond about $75,000 a year in the United States, more money does not buy any more happiness at all for the average US citizen earning above this amount. Being richer might make you **think** you are happier, but it does not necessarily make you **feel** any happier.'
>
> **Dolan, 2014**

Similarly, research done at Princeton University in 2006 suggested that the belief high income is associated with good mood is widespread but mostly illusory. [7]

Paul Dolan suggests that the happiest profession is gardening, and that the least happy is banking. Perhaps gardeners are happier because they have a clear sense of purpose and find a sense of Flow in what they do. Florists often (but not always) deal with people at happy points in their lives: when they are in love, want to say thank you or are getting married. Happiness – and unhappiness – are infectious.

For many of us, therefore, if you want to be happier in your life as a whole, solely pursuing the attainment of more money is unlikely to increase your happiness once you have enough for the basics in your life. This is not the expression of my personal philosophy but what the research shows – and it is in line with my own experience of life.

---

7. Quinones, 2006

Money, but at what cost? And the story of a very rich, very happy person

My mother, observing a relative, who was working extremely hard to establish his own business at considerable cost to his family relationships and his health, said, dryly, "He will be the richest man in the cemetery."

When I consider how many very rich people – and I have got to know quite a few over the years – I have met who I would consider to be very happy, the answer is one, who I met many years ago. Whilst a student, I was travelling coast to coast in the USA and had arrived at San Francisco, where I was to be introduced to a very wealthy lady by my elder brother, who had made a similar trip some years earlier. When she met me off the Greyhound coach, on which I had just travelled some three thousand miles in the last few days, she said: "I guess that you would like a shower and a steak." I thought to myself that we were likely to get on very well.

When we arrived at her enormous flat in central San Francisco and I had showered she showed me round her collection of wonderful artworks, which covered the very large wall area. "Which ones do you like most?" she asked (and suggested that my answer showed good taste).

The next day she invited me to an enormous party, where were gathered a fascinating collection of individuals: students, landscape gardeners, political activists, artists, well-travelled and well-read individuals. It was a great evening.

The next evening, she took me to one of the first shows of *Hair* – a great show, albeit highly controversial at the time.

Reflecting on the couple of days I had spent in her company, I thought that she was using her money to enjoy herself and collect interesting people whose company she enjoyed.

This was in stark contrast to other wealthy people I have met before and since who seemed to me to be often:

- obsessed with work to the exclusion of friends and family relationships
- unclear about who their real friends were and whether people just appeared to like them because they were rich
- anxious, often obsessive individuals
- having little or no time to savour the simple, pleasurable experiences that life provides if we put effort into finding them and take the time to enjoy them.

Achieving higher levels of well-being needs work: Just thinking positive thoughts will not make you happy or find you the right job

Positive thinking is indeed powerful but *just thinking positively is unlikely to change your life very much for the better*. To be happier in work and in your life as a whole you will need to:

1. Have a good understanding of yourself and your unique skills and motivations.
2. Be aware of and understand trends that affect your working life and their implications for you.
3. Be persistent in your efforts to identify and exploit advertised opportunities and those that your friends and colleagues can point you towards.
4. Be well prepared, positive and energetic and communicate well the unique contribution you can make to an organisation's needs.
5. Keep listening to feedback and adapting successfully.

You will also need to actually do these things on a day-to-day basis and not just have a vague and medium-term aspiration.

Happiness also makes organisations more profitable

As I mentioned at the beginning, well-being is not a zero-sum game – if you are happy, it does not mean that your organisation is losing out. On the contrary, organisations with a highly engaged workforce (i.e. where more people are happier) tend to be more profitable.

On average, business units in the top quartile on the employee engagement measure produced between 1 – 4 percentage points higher profitability (return on sales) (Harter, Schmidt and Keyes, 2003.)

According to Jessica Pryce-Jones,[8] happier employees are also up to 47% more productive.

Despite the old saying: "We don't pay you to enjoy yourself", organisations should have a strong interest in ensuring that their workforce is engaged, and individuals are happy in their work, because organisations with an engaged workforce are more profitable.

Pulling it together: The concept of "Ikigai" – your reason for being

A concept that I, and many of my clients, find helpful is the Japanese concept of Ikigai – your reason for being – that one of my clients, Denise, helpfully brought to my attention.

The basic idea is:

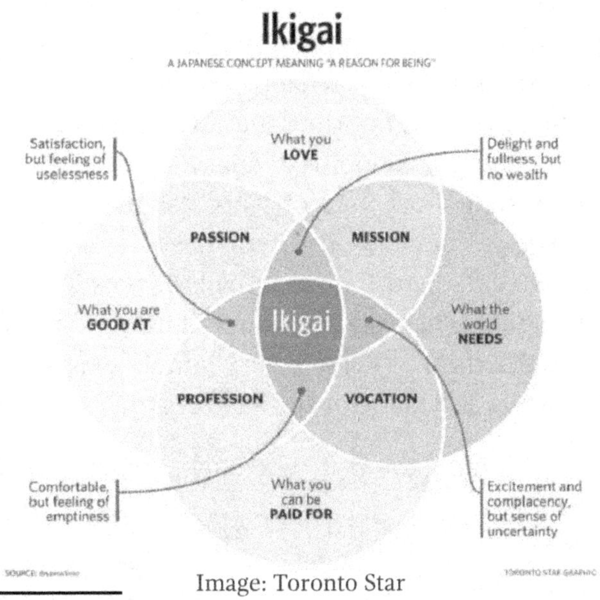

Image: Toronto Star

---

8. 2010

This is a sophisticated and, I think, elegant concept because it helps you consider not only what you are good at and what you can be paid for, but also what you love and what the world needs. In working with clients, I often encourage them to consider not only their profession but also the broader issues of what they love doing and what the world needs i.e. to move more from the bottom left of the diagram towards the centre. If you find you are in this central position (Ikigai) and work there, I believe that you will not only be good at what you do and be happy doing it, but you are likely to get encouraging feedback because what you are doing is something that the world needs – and people will notice and appreciate the passion you bring to your subject.

An exercise for you: What *does* make you happy?

Paul Dolan[9] believes that your happiness is determined by how you *allocate your attention.* As he points out, what you *think* should make you happy and what *actually* makes you happy are often not the same thing. To find out, you can try keeping a Happiness Diary. Every night, for a month, make a short note of what has made you happy and unhappy that day. You will need to do this daily because we can distort what actually makes us happy by thinking about what *should* make us happy – and they are not the same thing. This is a very simple exercise, but it is worthwhile and some of the answers may surprise you.

Without thinking about it too much, late each evening, make a note of:

---

9. 2014

1. What, in the last twenty-four hours, actually made you feel happy?
2. What, in the last twenty-four hours, actually made you feel unhappy?

The answers may be quite small events. Maybe:

- You enjoyed an ice cream or the look of a day in spring.
- Someone was particularly polite or said thank you.
- You made some progress on a long-term project that you had been postponing.
- You spent some time with a friend that you enjoyed.
- You made progress with a skill or a hobby that gave you some satisfaction.
- You enjoyed a workout at the gym.
- Something that you had felt was not in control became more in control.
- You gave someone time, advice or money and felt good about it.
- You realised that something you had been worrying about was not something you had to continue worrying about quite as much.
- You planned a holiday.
- A job interview went well.

I suggest that you don't try and analyse this very much during the month but at the end of the month, have a careful look through your notes and work out what conclusions you can draw.

1. In the previous month, what are the things that actually made you feel happy?
2. Are there situations in the last month in which you thrived? Situations that brought out the best in you? What are they? Why did you thrive?
3. In the previous month, are there work related things that made you unhappy?
4. To what extent are these things within your control, at least to some degree? (If they are really not under your control, maybe you should change jobs.)
5. Are there some changes that you might make to your life and/or work, even if it took some time and effort, that would help you experience the things that make you feel happy more often?
6. When you look at your happiness diary for the last month, does what actually made you happy bear any relationship to the above research? What can you learn from that?
7. What lessons can you learn from your diary about what you would like to do in future? What will you do differently tomorrow from yesterday?
8. Considering the things that persistently made you unhappy, what lessons can you learn? What changes can you make in the short or medium terms that would probably make you less unhappy?

9. In considering all of the above, what is the one thing you will start with and build more into your life? You should start with one small thing and start today.

A variation: the energy diary

Another approach (for which I am indebted to Emma West, leadership coach and non-executive director) is for you to keep an Energy Diary. You can carefully look back at your appointments, activities and particular people you spent time with over the previous month and decide which of these *gave you energy* and which of those *drained energy from you*. You will gain some important insights about what you actually enjoy and find energising and what you don't. You might prepare for some surprises: some of those things that you might feel you *should* enjoy on reflection you actually find draining and some of those perhaps very small things that you don't often think about, you actually derive a lot of energy and pleasure from. (I am usually very careful and tend to pause when I hear clients use the word "should" because it often means "won't" i.e. clients feel there is some social pressure bearing upon them, but they actually feel differently. It is considering how you *actually* feel that is likely to be more important in your future well-being.)

It might well be that you also realise that there are certain people, or types of people, that energise you or drain energy from you and so, in thinking about your future, you can consider how you can spend more time with people who energise you and less with those who don't.

The important principle here is that you consider what you *actually* enjoy, not what you or others think you *should* enjoy.

Conclusions

The main conclusions that we can now draw from the research about what makes people happier and more effective are:

1. Happy individuals are likely to live a decade longer, live healthier lives and be more productive.
2. How happy we are is quite substantially – 40% – within our control (50% of our overall level of well-being is a result of our genetic inheritance and only 10% is due to the particular circumstances of our upbringing).
3. There is strong evidence from the Government Office for Science that we can increase our level of happiness by:

    a. Working with an organisation whose sense of **purpose** we identify with.

    b. **Investing in relationships** and connecting with those around us.

    c. Being **active** – finding a form of exercise that we enjoy and practising it regularly.

    d. **Taking notice of the present:** live in and savour the moment. Meditation reduces the effect of stress on your DNA.

e. **Keep learning:** try something new.

f. **Giving:** Seeing yourself, and your happiness, as linked to the wider community can be incredibly rewarding and creates connections with the people around you.

4. It is not all about money: once we have enough income to cover our basic needs, more money is unlikely to make most of us happier.
5. Adversity can make us stronger and more resilient.
6. We will have to *work* at being happy to become happier – thinking positive thoughts is not enough.
7. By working to be happier in our work we are not being selfish; organisations with engaged workforces are more profitable.

One overall interesting conclusion is also that happiness does not cost money – it is more a question of having the right knowledge, attention and attitude, and then working hard at increasing your level of well-being in a way that works for you as an individual.

In short, the evidence about what makes most of us happy and fulfilled, and the substantial benefits to us in terms of both our health and productivity, is very compelling. It is up to us to improve our overall level of happiness, and notwithstanding the fact that we will experience challenges and setbacks, research shows clearly how we can work to be happier in both our lives as a whole and in our work. Over to you!

CHAPTER 2

Learning from Your Past

Turning points: You had better stop what you are doing

I had been pedalling hard on the exercise bike for a few minutes. The doctor looked at the blood pressure gauge and said: "We won't be continuing the exercise test today, Mr. Smith."

I had been working as a company doctor – going into companies that were in financial trouble and trying to sort them out and give them a future as a temporary chief executive. On several occasions I was in a position where if I did not reach agreement with the banks to carry on supporting the company by 3.00 p.m. that afternoon, the next morning I would be telling more than 1,000 people they were almost certainly unemployed. Thankfully, all the companies I worked with survived and went on to have a future.

The work was satisfying – it felt good when the patient company survived – but it could be very stressful. I was mindful of the fact that my father had died of a brain haemorrhage when I was aged twelve, and so, after I had been working as a company doctor for about six years, I thought it would be a good idea for me to have a thorough medical check-up.

That day on the exercise bike was the moment I discovered that my blood pressure was high – high enough to make me think that I did not want to die in my fifties like my father.

I began to think seriously about my future: what I could do, what I could be paid to do and what I wanted to do.

Eight years earlier I had been working in New Zealand, developing international power generation projects, when all the Asian economies had crashed simultaneously, and I had come back to the UK. As part of my leaving package, I was offered and accepted career transition support in central London. As I had found the service and advice very helpful, it occurred to me that one of the things I could do would be to become a coach for executives in career transition, i.e. between jobs. I had worked in four different countries, in many different sectors and in a wide variety of roles. I liked to think I was a good listener and could give sensible advice.

And so, a few days after my medical had been aborted, I called the career transition unit I had previously worked with. To my surprise, the office manager remembered me as a client from eight years earlier and suggested that I come and have a chat with the managing partner. A few days later I did, and we agreed that I should give it a try – after sitting in client sessions with very experienced coaches so that I could learn the ropes.

Since then, I have worked with more than 300 executives, at different levels of seniority, from a very wide range of backgrounds and nationalities and in a very wide range of personal circumstances. Some of them have been quite depressed and some of them have had high media profiles – some negative. I have tried to help all of them work out what they most wanted in their working lives and then helped them achieve their goals, the vast majority of whom have done so successfully.

To be told that you have made a real difference for the better in your clients' lives (I have got my dream job!) after accompanying them on what was often a quite difficult and unpredictable journey, is very satisfying. When they get where they want to go, we had (pre-pandemic) a custom of buying them lunch to celebrate, which was usually a real pleasure for both of us. Most of this book is what I have learnt from working with them.

The underlying question has always been the same for me: what role (or collection of roles) will this individual in front of me be best at and be most happy doing? What is the evidence from their lives so far that supports this view? The answers are often quite surprising and the exploration can be fun, if a bit scary for the client.

This is why, having asked and answered that question more than 300 times in my work with individual clients, I became interested in trying to understand the evidence from research about the broader question of what *actually* makes people happy and effective in their work? Does well-being matter in terms of both the individuals' health and organisational profitability? Are there things individuals can do to increase the odds that they will be happier and more effective in their working lives?

Having read widely about the answers to these questions – and we do increasingly know a great deal about the answers – I thought I would enjoy sharing what I have learnt more widely. Hence this book, which is built around what we know about work and well-being and how we can each be happier and more effective in our working lives – and hence our lives as a whole. I am now sharing this experience and knowledge, partly because research shows that for most people, sharing and giving is more satisfying than taking – and so it is for me.

I had not known, when the doctor told me to stop pedalling on the exercise bike, that this would dramatically change more than the next twelve years of my life. With hindsight, it was one of the most important turning points in my working life.

Why does well-being matter in your working life?

Welcome to your adventure of designing and creating your preferred working future!

I approach this subject from the point of view of well-being as well as considering the practicalities that can help you on your journey. The thing I like most about well-being is that being happy and effective in your job is not a zero-sum game – everyone can win. Remember that if you are happy and effective in what you do you are likely to:

- Live a decade longer and have a healthier life
- Be up to 47% more productive
- If most of your colleagues are also relatively happy,

you are more likely to be working for a more productive and profitable organisation.

This is why it is worthwhile putting effort into learning about what sort of role(s) you will be best suited to and then learning how to improve your chances of obtaining the right role(s) for you.

Learning from your past

In this chapter I will encourage you to explore what you can learn from your past:

- What you can learn from key turning points you have identified in your past working life and what do they tell you about what is really important to you.
- I start with what the low points in your working life can tell you. Perhaps when you have had low points you discovered that you are more resilient and adaptable than you previously thought and what had been a very tough period at the time really helped you in your later working life.
- Thinking about the high points in your working life can also give you key insights because they will suggest what really matters to you and therefore give you important clues about the type of role and organisation you are most likely to thrive in.
- Exercises you can do to capture this learning so that you can benefit from it in the future.
- What conclusions you can draw about learning from your past.

What did I learn from my own past?

In working out what would be a good working future for you, you should consider lessons from your past that have been important in your working life. My episode on the exercise bike was an important turning point for me because it made me realise that:

- If I carried on doing the work I was doing (that of a company doctor) it might lead me to an early death like my father.
- Having developed high blood pressure, I would be wise to listen to my body and start taking the signs seriously.
- I needed to change the work I was doing quite dramatically in order to try to find ways of spending my time in a job I enjoyed, which I had the skills to do well and which would pay me enough to live on.

Some thinking for you to do: low points

You will almost certainly have experienced, perhaps more clearly with hindsight, some important turning points in your life, which will be very different from mine. They may have been negative in the short term but might have since had more positive long-term consequences. Perhaps:

- You made a stand on an issue that was very important for you – and there were negative consequences.
- You were given some blunt advice from someone you respected that made you think about what you really wanted to do with your life.

- You made an important error of judgement.
- You had a life experience (e.g. an accident) not directly related to work, which had significant consequences for your working life.
- Someone close to you died and you had to change the work you did.
- You were unexpectedly fired.
- You discovered you had a serious health issue, which meant you had to change direction.
- You had to change where you lived to look after an ageing parent or ill partner.
- It became obvious that you would no longer be paid for work you were familiar with because of changes in your company's or organisation's circumstances.
- You realised that you simply could not stand the work you were doing any longer and had to change your job.
- You could not get on with your boss and felt that he/she could not get on with you.
- You were under such pressure that you did not feel in control of your life.
- You really didn't like the politics of your organisation – some people seem to put nearly all their efforts into looking good rather than doing good.
- You felt out of your depth and didn't feel confident enough to ask for help.

- You did not like the values of your organisation – although it said nice things in the annual report about the company's values you could see from the actual behaviour from the bosses and the people around you that the *actual* values, expressed through behaviour, were quite different, and you did not agree with them.
- The pressure to keep on doing more and more with less and less was just impossible. You felt burnt out.
- You might have suffered bullying or racial or sexual discrimination.
- Despite your best efforts, you just did not feel valued or fairly rewarded.

It will be helpful for you to identify a few important turning points in your life so that by understanding more about your past you can more effectively prepare to create a better working future. Identify your own turning points, answer these questions and think about what they tell you about how you might be happier in your future working life.

One way in which you can do this is to draw a line that represents all of your working life so far. The graph of your working life – or *Lifeline* – will go up at the high points – where you have felt most fulfilled and happy – and down at your low points – where you have felt most bored, frustrated, angry, undervalued, or ineffective. Concentrate on:

1. *key turning points* – where, with hindsight, your working life changed significantly

2. *the highest and the lowest* points in your career so far. Remember in some detail what was happening during each of them.

Turning points

Having identified some key turning points in your life, consider each one. You can use the space below to make notes.

Turning point 1:

a. What happened?

....
....
....
....
....

b. Why did it happen?

....
....
....
....
....

c. How did you feel about it at the time?

....
....
....
....
....

d. If you were watching this turning point as a scene in movie, what advice would you now give yourself as the key character?

....

....

....

....

....

e. If you could relive that period, what would you have done, or avoided doing, differently?

....

....

....

....

....

f. With the benefit of hindsight, what have you now learnt from this turning point?

....

....

....

....

....

g. How did that turning point go on to change your life?

....

....

....

....

....

h. What did it tell you about what is really important to you?

....

....

....

....

....

i. What are the implications for your preferred future working life? How should what you have learnt from your turning points influence your choices about your future?

....

....

....

....

....

Turning point 2:

a. What happened?

b. Why did it happen?

c. How did you feel about it at the time?

d. If you were watching this turning point as a scene in movie, what advice would you now give yourself as the key character?

e. If you could relive that period, what would you have done, or avoided doing, differently?

....

....

....

....

....

f. With the benefit of hindsight, what have you now learnt from this turning point?

....

....

....

....

....

g. How did that turning point go on to change your life?

....

....

....

....

....

h. What did it tell you about what is really important to you?

....

....

....

....

....

i. What are the implications for your preferred future working life? How should what you have learnt from your turning points influence your choices about your future?

....

....

....

....

....

Turning point 3:

a. What happened?

....

....

....

....

....

b. Why did it happen?

....

....

....

....

....

c. How did you feel about it at the time?

....

....

....

....

....

d. If you were watching this turning point as a scene in movie, what advice would you now give yourself as the key character?

....

....

....

....

....

e. If you could relive that period, what would you have done, or avoided doing, differently?

....

....

....

....

....

f. With the benefit of hindsight, what have you now learnt from this turning point?

....

....

....

....

....

g. How did that turning point go on to change your life?

....

....

....

....

....

h. What did it tell you about what is really important to you?

....

....

....

....

....

i. What are the implications for your preferred future working life? How should what you have learnt from your turning points influence your choices about your future?

....

....

....

....

....

Low points: The yellow plastic bucket – and a lesson about resilience

One set of experiences for you to consider are the low points of your career so far, which will tell you lessons about your future. Here is one of the low points from my career.

Times were hard. When I was a student, we experienced the three-day week – because of widespread national strikes there was no electricity for two days each week. Television companies were instructed to stop broadcasting at 10.30 p.m. to conserve electricity and hospitals could only deal with emergency patients. My student friends showed their sense of humour by putting up posters: "Save electricity, bathe with a friend!" The gravediggers later went on strike and so bodies were not being buried. The whole population of the UK was very polarised by the long running, bitter and violent miners' strike. The election slogan was: "Who runs Britain?" i.e. the trades unions or the government.

A few years later I was in my first general management job in an international lighting company after completing my

MBA (we were fondly known as Masters of Bugger All). My part of the company was making sixty-four million light bulbs per annum but was incurring substantial financial losses, not least because industrial relations at our three factories were truly awful. I had recently negotiated and won two sole-supply lighting contracts to bring more work to the factories and I had introduced Total Quality Management (what might now be called Lean or Agile ways of working) techniques to improve customer service, make jobs more interesting and improve the company's financial performance.

One of the smallest changes we made was in the use of a yellow plastic bucket with which to move thousands of lighting filament wires from one end of the production line to the other in order to improve productivity. A trades union official had greeted this change with the comment: "That will be new technology, Mr. Smith," i.e. he wanted a pay raise for his members in return for using a yellow plastic bucket – when the company was losing money and when its whole future was at risk. Then at the busiest time of our production year, the unions declared an overtime ban, which meant that we would almost certainly lose our two largest sole-supply contracts, and this would probably result in the closure of the factory with the loss of six hundred jobs. The situation was desperately difficult.

We studied examples of change management in companies in the local area and the lesson from them was that all the local companies who had been very reasonable and consultative had failed. The only ones who had succeeded had developed aggressive change management plans along the lines of: "I am your new boss, this is the way it is going to be, I hope you will join us".

I had therefore developed a radical change management plan and tried to sell it to my boss. He could see, rightly, that there would be significant risks in implementing my plan given the history of difficult industrial relations. I had the support of the factory management and had even lined up the money necessary to build a new factory that would use world-class technology, but I could not persuade my boss to support my plan and sadly concluded, “I don’t have any other ideas”.

Not long afterwards, he told me that he had decided to make me redundant, and commented: “I don’t know why I did not do this earlier”. An incoming senior manager carried on with the pursuit of total quality techniques and observed: “I am surprised you are still here”.

The finance director, who was one of the individuals I had personally made redundant but with whom I got on with very well, wrote me a handwritten letter of support, saying that he did not know how I did it, i.e. remain positive and professional when I had four young children and had just been fired. I had subsequently offered to buy the company as I felt I could give it a better future but was told it was not for sale. A few years later the company was sadly closed down – not sold – as it was felt it was not viable.

I then spent less than twelve months in a group headquarters role and joined a large electricity company as a main board Plc director where I was responsible for one billion pounds of sales, six thousand people and trying to change a monopoly government-owned body into a highly competitive company with excellent customer service. It seems natural to us now that customers can choose their electricity supplier, but all the companies at that time were monopoly publicly-owned suppliers. Customers who, without irony, were referred to as Applicants at the time, were then able to choose who would supply their electricity for the first time ever.

One lesson I learnt from that very difficult experience was I was quite resilient. It was far from easy, but I had gone on to do a much larger and even more challenging job than I had had in the lighting company. This was largely because I simply *had* to do it; you don't reflect too much about what you might do when you have four young mouths to feed, you just get on and do it. (Research shows that many people are much more resilient than they think.)

You might also find it helpful to remember that so far, you have a 100% survival rate from your bad days!

Learning from your low points

Having identified some low points in your career so far, what are the lessons for you?

1. What had happened to make you feel so bad?

   ....

   ....

   ....

   ....

   ....

2. Looking back, why do you think it happened? Could you have done anything differently that would have made things less bad?

   ....

   ....

   ....

   ....

   ....

3. What were the factors that made the situation intolerable?

   ....

   ....

   ....

   ....

   ....

4. Complete the sentence: I will now always look for a situation where I am able to ...

   ....

   ....

   ....

   ....

   ....

5. What are the negative aspects of this experience you can turn into positive qualities in organisations and roles that you should look for? e.g. if your work-life balance had been put under intolerable pressure previously, how can you reduce the risk of that happening again? As part of your research before taking a job you could review what employees say about what it is actually like to work

in this organisation before you seriously consider joining them (e.g. check out Glassdoor, ask former employees).

....

....

....

....

....

6. After moving on from this low point, what actually happened? Did you move onto a role or different organisation where the problems were not as bad? Did you take the lessons you had learnt into account? In the long run, did that negative experience help you? Did you learn something about how resilient you could be in difficult circumstances? What helped you to do this?

....

....

....

....

....

Learning from your high points: One hundred and thirty million people

After graduating with a second-class degree in English and French I had volunteered for Voluntary Service Overseas (VSO) and was posted to Indonesia for two years. (In those days you could express a preference for where you might be posted but you were actually posted to wherever the need was greatest.) Knowing nothing at the time about Indonesia, I soon learnt that it was the fifth largest country in the world with a population (then) of 130 million spread over 17,000 islands and with over 300 languages.

I then spent two years teaching English to university graduates and civil servants in central Java so that they could go abroad to study in their professional field and return to work in senior roles in the Indonesian government, which nearly all of them did.

A couple of years later, I went on to work for an American philanthropic organisation that worked to develop Indonesian capabilities in fields that were important for successful economic and environmental development. For three years I was working inside the Indonesian Government, designing and then running a small unit that selected Indonesian civil servants and academics for international study in fields such as agricultural economics, forest management, river basin management or marine ecology. I had become something of an expert in how to get good candidates through the labyrinthine Indonesian bureaucracy and find them funding for foreign study before they came back to work in important roles in Indonesia and made a contribution to their country's development.

One day, I was asked by my boss if I would like to join a project being run by the World Bank. They were concerned that Indonesia was one of their biggest borrowers but did not seem to have enough management capacity to run large environmental projects and so they wanted to develop an approach that would allow Indonesia to develop the right quantity and quality of management to run this type of project successfully. They were expecting to spend some $300 million (in 1980's money) implementing their recommendations and so help the fifth largest country in the world manage their most difficult environmental problems. (This was in 1980, long before environmental concerns become mainstream!)

And so, at the age of twenty-nine, I joined the small project team (the Mission) that had been put together – everyone else on the team was a subject area specialist and was based in Washington. The Mission was to last just six weeks. My role, knowing as I did by then a great deal about how to get Indonesians trained on a global basis, was to advise the World Bank how they might best spend some $300 million on training Indonesian specialists in environmental management subjects. The team started by interviewing the Indonesian ministers of agriculture, the environment and education minister, and then working down the government structures, gathering views and evidence as we went.

I wrote my part of the report, which advised the Indonesian Government what to do in order to develop the capability to manage environmental projects successfully over the next thirty years.

In participating in this project team, I had:

- used a high level of skill and my knowledge of how the Indonesian Government worked in a very short time period with a very intelligent, knowledgeable and committed World Bank project team
- developed a very high sense of purpose – I was helping the fifth largest country in the world develop expertise that would help solve some of its most important environmental problems that would directly affect the lives of 130 million people (now over 300 million) for several generations
- obtained rapid feedback (the recommendations were basically accepted).

Even though I did this work more than forty years ago, and only for a period of six weeks, it is still one of the things I feel most proud of contributing to in my working life. (You will have learnt from Chapter 1 that this is a good example of what is called a Flow experience.)

Learning from your high points

Nearly all of us have high points in our careers and they will be very particular to you and your own experience and circumstances. What they have in common is that whenever they occurred, they still make you feel good or proud. Perhaps:

- Someone asked your advice, you had a discussion and introduced them to someone who was really able to help with the next step of their career.

- You worked with a team of people who you enjoyed working with and accomplished something that most of your colleagues had said would be impossible.
- You saw something – an opportunity, insight or potential solution – that no one else had seen, and then made it happen.
- You worked on something that you felt made a real contribution to solving a difficult problem.
- You really felt that the work you were doing was changing people's lives for the better.
- Your boss said that you had done a brilliant piece of work.
- You were working with an organisation that had a strong sense of values that you really agreed with.
- Having trained and practised for a long period you found that you could do something that you had never been able to do before and that people really appreciated what you could do.
- Someone you respected said thank you and sounded as if they meant it.
- Your boss expressed confidence in you that you could do the job, even though you had not done it before.

Your high points will be very particular to you, and very different from mine, but you can learn a lot from them in a way that should affect future choices you will make.

1. From the whole of your working life to date, what are your particular high points?

   ....
   ....
   ....
   ....
   ....

2. What were you doing, what skills were you using, with what sort of people and with what sense of purpose?

   ....
   ....
   ....
   ....
   ....

3. Why are they high points for you?

   ....
   ....
   ....
   ....
   ....

4. What is it, in particular, that makes you feel proud about this high point?

   ....
   ....
   ....
   ....
   ....

5. What type of risks did you take to achieve your goals? What does this suggest about the type of risks you might take in the future?

   ....

   ....

   ....

   ....

   ....

6. What sort of feedback did you receive and how quickly?

   ....

   ....

   ....

   ....

   ....

7. How were you rewarded? Was it mainly that you knew yourself that you had done a good job? Was your achievement recognised? Looking back, what was the most important reward? Was it something other than money?

   ....

   ....

   ....

   ....

   ....

8. What can you learn from them in terms of the type of work you have most enjoyed and found most fulfilling?

   ....

   ....

   ....

   ....

   ....

9. Complete the sentence: In the future I will really look out for situations where [...] because I find these most satisfying.

   ....

   ....

   ....

   ....

   ....

If you complete these exercises thoughtfully (possibly discussing them with your partner or a trusted friend or colleague) you will already be much better equipped to search out the type of role in the type of organisation that will be likely to help you be happier – and do a much better job – than you were previously.

Conclusions

1. Consciously reflecting on what have been the most important turning points in your working life so far will help you understand what is really important to you.
2. Turning points are things that you should not ignore in planning the next stage of your working

life because they will have played an important role in determining who you are and what you can offer a future employer. If they were key turning points for you, you are also quite unlikely to be able to change those aspects of your personality and values that gave rise to them so you should look for a place where you can use these motivations, skills, and experience to good effect.

3. It is equally important to consider both the high and low points of your working life so far, because of what they tell you about you, your values, how you behave in certain situations and those situations in the future that you should either really try to avoid or those to which you would be very well suited and highly motivated by. Your low points may have helped you understand that you are more resilient than you thought.
4. Having reflected on your turning points, the high and low points of your working life so far, you should work through the above exercises so that you have consciously learnt lessons that will help shape your preferred working life.

Chapter 3

Who Do You Think You Are?

Now you better understand what, from research, is likely to make you happier and you have consciously learnt from your past, you can begin to think about what an ideal role(s) would be for you. In thinking about what sort of role you would most like to have in the next part of your working life, it is important that you try and see yourself from the perspective of your next potential employer i.e. rather objectively. Answering these questions is an exercise that will help you do this. (It will also help you begin to prepare for interviews, which we will discuss in more detail in Chapter 12.)

1. **Tell me about yourself.** How would you describe yourself in a couple of paragraphs, or even better, several sentences, from the perspective of an organisation that might think of employing you? This should not be a detailed account of all the stages of your curriculum vitae (CV) but more a

very short summary of what you would be "bringing to the party" as a new employee.

....

....

....

....

....

....

....

2. **What are your main areas of skills and experience?** Can you summarise the main areas of skills that you have developed? These may be formal or professional qualifications or your strongest areas of experience in one or more sectors. They are subject areas in which you feel confident.

....

....

....

....

....

....

....

3. **How would your colleagues describe you?** If I were to talk to several of your colleagues, what sort of words would they realistically use to describe you? Try and think of what they have actually said. A definition I quite like is that "Brand You" is what people say about you when you are not in the room. What might they say on a bad day? This might include positive and less positive characteristics, because it is important that you try and avoid

situations and roles that have previously resulted in you not being at your best, or where you have been the subject of (mainly fair) criticism.

....

....

....

....

....

....

....

4. **Your recent achievements.** A potential employer will, of course, want to know what you have been responsible for, but what they will be more interested in is what you personally did and what difference you actually made. What have you done that has made you proud in the last five years? Try and think of about five achievements so that you can choose which are the best ones to present at interview. (Situation, Task, Action, Result – STAR performance.)

   ....

   ....

   ....

   ....

   ....

   ....

   ....

5. **Motivations.** When have you been highly motivated and energised? What are the circumstances in which this happened? Equally important, what has stopped you from being at your best? Given this,

what type of circumstances should you try and avoid in future? What type of role would really excite you? As above, it is a good rule of thumb in exploring potential opportunities for you to *follow your energy*. If a type of role or boss would make you feel motivated and energised, you are much more likely to be good in it. Unless you absolutely have no choice, you should not pursue something unless it excites you. If you are not motivated on day one, you are unlikely to have the resilience to overcome the challenges you will certainly experience in the future.

....

....

....

....

....

....

....

6. **Feedback.** What feedback have you had from colleagues that is reasonably consistent? What are the implications of this in terms of what you should be looking for in your next role?

....

....

....

....

....

....

....

7. **Relationships.** What type of people do you usually get on well with? Are there examples of individuals you have not worked well with? Does this tell you anything about the type of boss or colleagues that you should ideally be looking for? Are there any lessons from working relationships that have been very difficult in terms of what you should try and avoid in future?

   ....

   ....

   ....

   ....

   ....

   ....

   ....

8. **Working environment: culture.** There may well be types of organisations or cultures that you work very well in – perhaps where you have a lot of freedom to get on with the job or perhaps where the purpose of the organisation you are working for is one you feel strongly positive about – make a note of them. And there may well be types of organisations where you would not work well, e.g. where there is a strong blame culture, where you would be very closely supervised or where you might have concerns about the ethics of the organisation.

You should therefore try and find out what is the actual culture of the organisation you are considering working for or being interviewed by. (It is quite often forgotten that when an organisation is interviewing candidates it is selling as well as buying. Strong candidates are likely to have choices and if they gain a negative impression of their potential employer during the selection process, they are likely to go elsewhere). During the selection process you should be actively looking for clues about what it is actually like to work there and thinking about whether this is the type of organisation you would be very happy to work for. If you have a chance to explore this further e.g., by talking confidentially to ex-employees, looking at what people say on Glassdoor or visiting the work site informally, you should do so.

....

....

....

....

....

....

....

9. **How mobile are you?** Where would you be happy to consider working? Obviously, the smaller the geographic area you would consider, the fewer opportunities there will be. Would you consider working internationally? Which regions of the world would you consider working in and which not?

Moving internationally would be a big decision for you to take and would have significant impacts on your family and social life, but it might give you a professional, social, and cultural experience that you would enjoy, and which would be likely to be attractive to potential future employers because you have demonstrated your ability to work well in a very different environment.

....

....

....

....

....

....

....

10. **What's the deal?** Having considered your financial needs (which is obviously not the same as what you would *ideally* like) you will have a view about what base salary and benefits would be the minimum you could sensibly accept (on the big assumption that you have a reasonable degree of choice). You might exercise some degree of flexibility about your package if you are really excited about what the organisation actually does.

The best time to negotiate your package is after you know that the organisation has taken the decision that they would like to employ you. This is when you will have the most bargaining power. Depending on the circumstances, the organisation will have more or less flexibility in terms of what they can offer you. In any case, you will have more negotiating power just before you commit to joining the organisation than you are likely to have once you have started work there.

As organisations recruit post-pandemic, you should try to have a discussion about what is the degree of flexibility in your working arrangements, e.g. are there times and days that you will be required to be in the office? What is the degree of flexibility in these arrangements so that they are likely to suit your circumstances? How can you be in more control of your working life? Can you discuss and agree a form of hybrid or flexible working that could work well for you and your employer? Are you comfortable with their policies on hybrid work patterns? (See Chapter 6 on Flexible Working.)

....

....

....

....

....

....

....

Your options

Depending on your financial circumstances, if you have given some time to thinking about what type of role in what type of organisation you would ideally like to be offered, you may find you have a broader range of options than you might have imagined. Now you are considering what you would like to do next, you should take every advantage of this opportunity to identify a role that you would really enjoy and then very actively look for it. If you are really excited about your new job, you will almost certainly be a better employee for your new organisation and so you are not being selfish in reflecting on this carefully. You can discuss what you see as your options with friends and colleagues and see if their perspective about what would work best for you is similar to yours or whether you should see things a bit differently in the light of your discussions with them.

How much freedom you have to choose your ideal role in practice, is likely to vary quite a lot over the course of your career. If you have no job, young children, a substantial mortgage and not very much by way of savings, you will need to find another job urgently and not have too much time for self-reflection. Later in your career, perhaps after you have paid off the mortgage and you no longer have to support your children financially, you might have much more scope to come to conclusions about what you would actually most like to do, and your experience is likely to be of greater value to employers.

One role or more than one? The portfolio career

Up to now I have generally assumed that you are looking for a single new job. In working with clients over the last decade, however, one trend that I have seen is that an increasing number of clients, even during what would usually be thought of as when they are mid-career, are thinking of having more than one role – of having a portfolio career. This is an important decision. It might be that you could work for several different organisations at the same time. (You will need to become skilled at managing your diary!) This might give you more satisfaction as your working week will be much more varied. It might actually also be lower risk because if one of those roles does not work out you still have another two or three that are providing you with income until you find another part-time role to fill the gap. This is also likely to leave you in more control of your working life since you are not completely dependent on one organisation or one boss. I expect that this pattern of an increasing number of people looking for and holding several different roles earlier in their career will become more common.

In conclusion

By thinking carefully about these sorts of issues and answering the above questions you will be:

- better prepared for interviews and more persuasive in them
- more likely to enjoy your new job
- more likely to be successful in it.

This (slow) thinking time is therefore likely to be time very well spent.

Chapter 4

Creating Your Preferred Working Future

Take a Day at a Time or Plan?

My own career planning – a more opportunistic approach

"We are an old company getting younger, and we need people like you," said the middle-aged executive at the end of the table around which were seated five of my business postgraduate colleagues. We had all just graduated from business school and were attending a meeting with our employer-to-be, a large, highly diversified industrial company that was keen on hiring MBAs.

A few weeks earlier I had received a telex (yes, showing my age) from this organisation asking if I could come to an interview. I had replied apologetically that I was not available on the date proposed and had not expected to hear any more from them. Because they were a multi-billion-pound company, I expected the recruitment process would be extremely competitive and so I would probably have no chance of success because I had not been available for the first interview.

To my surprise, a few weeks later I received a second telex from them asking me to come to the second meeting that I was now attending. The company executive then proceeded to go round the table asking each of my colleagues what sort of role they would prefer to have in this large organisation.

By the time he had got halfway round the table the thought was going through my mind –they don't realise that I haven't been interviewed! A couple of minutes later, before I tried to give what I hoped was a plausible answer to his question, the second thought going through my mind was: In a company like this, there must be opportunities ...

I joined this company a few weeks later as a business planning manager, responsible for pulling together strategic business plans for six small engineering companies, a typical role for a newly qualified MBA at that time.

Eighteen months later, I was the only one of my fellow MBAs still employed by them (and was to stay there in a variety of roles for the next seven years) – each of my business school colleagues had left for one reason or another.

For much of my subsequent working life I tended to concentrate hard on the eighteen or so months in front of me, tried to fulfil the role required of me in the expectation that if I did it well, I would be likely to be asked to do something interesting subsequently, which often proved to be the case.

This is an example of an opportunistic approach – I had not planned for, or foreseen, the opportunity but grasped it successfully once it presented itself.

In terms of your approach to your future working life, you can take a relatively opportunistic approach – seeing what comes along and seizing the opportunity in front of you – or consciously take a more planned approach to the definition and creation of your future. Which approach works better for you will depend partly on your personality, but given the pace of change in the world of organisations and business (and your own priorities as they evolve), it is probably true to say that it is quite difficult to say reliably what sort of position you and your organisation will be in more than eighteen months or so into the future.

In this chapter we will consider:

- that an opportunistic approach is possible
- how the concept of a "career" is no longer very helpful because the nature of work is changing so quickly
- how you can alternatively think about and plan the next stage of your working life using David Cooper's Four Quadrant model – see page 105 (outer and inner world, hard to influence and able to influence)
- the importance of "boundary" issues in the model such as your motivation and values
- depending on your personality and the point at which you are at in your working life, if a more

opportunistic or planned approach may be better for you

- the approach that might work best in most cases may be to learn as much as possible about yourself and what you are best at so that you can either take advantage of opportunities as they come along or more consciously identify what you would most like to do and then proactively search for appropriate opportunities and prepare carefully for them
- how you begin to plan and act upon the decisions you can take to improve the odds of getting a role(s), that you are well suited to and are likely to enjoy.

Life is less predictable – the idea of a career is less useful than it was; limitations to planning

I tell the above story to illustrate that life is often gloriously unpredictable, and both opportunities and problems have a habit of just turning up, and we have to deal with them as best as we are able.

In the earlier stages of my career (I prefer to use the expression working life) – I tended not to try and plan my future as it was quite difficult for me to imagine what range of futures might exist and how I might try to create them. I also had young children to provide for and so I was *most* concerned about having *a* job (not quite any job) rather than trying to plan.

At the time I graduated from university in the 1980s, large businesses such as oil companies could offer potential employees a reasonably predictable pattern of employment that might last more than twenty years. If you stayed with the same organisation and did well, you would be expected to reach a certain rank or role, which could be pretty well predicted twenty years earlier. The deal was that the organisation more-or-less looked after its and your interests by taking decisions about your promotions (or lack of them) and in return you had stable and predictable employment.

The nature of work and organisations has since changed dramatically in the UK, and internationally, during the twentieth century. The notion of a job for life has almost completely disappeared – with the arguable/partial exceptions of the church, the army, large accounting or legal firms, and to a lesser degree, parts of the civil service.

I make this point because the notion of a career suggests that someone else is at least partially responsible for your future working life. Increasingly, I believe, *the only person responsible for your future working life is, and I believe, should be, you.*

I therefore think the notion of a career as a concept is largely obsolete and therefore an unhelpful way of thinking. In the past – when roles passed from father to son and when there were large, stable and hierarchical organisations – the notion of a career made sense. But in an age when we and organisations have to be more agile, and where command and control cultures and hierarchical structures have largely disappeared, I believe we need to find a different model, e.g. one that is able to take into account developments such as the gig economy, which is more about the intersection of markets of willing buyer and willing seller at any one time. (In one sense, we are all in the gig economy now.) This is quite different from the traditional legal concept of employer and employee, which is fundamentally based upon a master/servant relationship, (see Chapter 6 on flexible working).

In my lifetime, the degree of technologically led change has been quite extraordinary. The mainframe computer, the personal computer, the mobile phone, the internet, robotics, social media, big data and personalised medicine have all arrived – and the age of artificial intelligence is emerging very fast indeed. This all illustrates that the pace of change in our working lives is fast and getting faster and therefore that the future of your working life is very difficult to predict. Unforeseen events – the COVID-19 pandemic or Russia's invasion of Ukraine – also have a habit of turning any plans we might have upside down. It is therefore very likely that personal agility is going to be important in managing our future working lives.

If the idea of a stable and predictable career isn't very helpful, what might replace it? Are there ways in which we can usefully think about our working futures?

A more planned approach to your working life: The Four Quadrant Model (David Cooper)

Many of us may prefer to take a more planned approach to the definition of our preferred working future.

How can we usefully begin to think about our working future then? One way is to use the simple but profound model proposed by David Cooper that considers your future working life in terms of four quadrants: those parts of your working life that come from reflecting on what you could substantially change – and what you cannot change – and those parts of your life that come from within you (such as your basic personality and preferences) and those more external parts of your life (such as your working environment).

Life Planning: The Four Quadrant Model

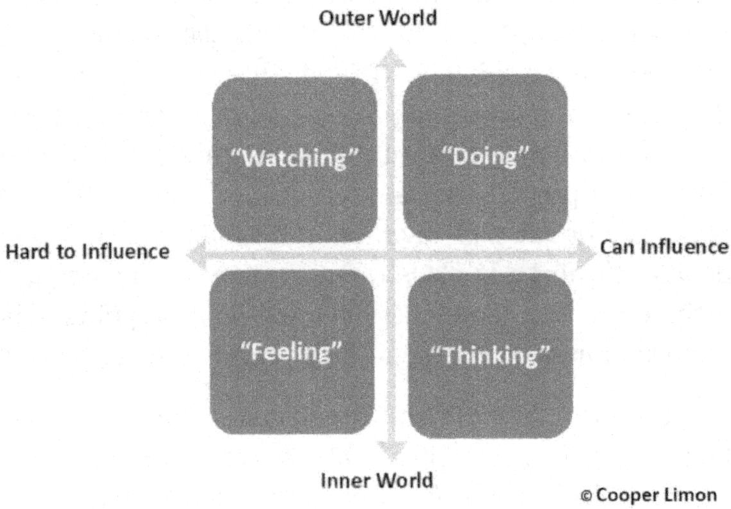

Let's consider each of the four quadrants:

Outer World – Hard to Influence: "Watching"

In this area, e.g. the level of demand for your type of skills, the economic environment, unemployment levels, Brexit, the COVID-19 pandemic, the effects of the war in Ukraine – it is unlikely that you will be able to influence this outer world significantly. It will not be helpful to be anxious or unduly concerned about these sorts of issues – because you can't change them – but it is important that you are broadly aware of them so that you can have an intelligent discussion about them at interview and so that you can use your knowledge of them to perform a sanity check on your aspirations. If, for example, you had a heartfelt desire to be a traditional black cab driver, you need to know that that world is changing rapidly and that there are some 40,000 Uber cab drivers in London who are self-employed and that is therefore making it a lot harder to earn a living in this way.

The sort of issues that lie in this quadrant are:

- relevant aspects of the economy and major political/policy issues
- what is happening in the job market that you are most interested in?
- what is the organisational agenda and culture of your target organisations?
- what is happening in the development of technologies that may be relevant to your area of work?

You will not be able to have much direct influence over these sorts of issues, but it is important that you are aware of them and take them into account.

So, the key word in this quadrant is "**Watching**" – being aware of what is happening in the area you are most interested in, even if you are not able to influence these events very much.

Inner World – Hard to Influence – "Feeling"

Some aspects of your personality – your inner world – will be relatively stable and hard to change. If during the last ten years you have insisted on running your own show, resented any form of supervision and been proud of what you have personally and uniquely created, it is likely that you will need a fair amount of autonomy in your next role. If you are considering working for a particular organisation, it would be a good idea for you to find out how much individual initiative is encouraged there. If you were to accept a role in an organisation, which has a culture that is incompatible with your basic personality and/or values, you are unlikely to thrive because you cannot – and may in any case may not want to – change the stable and long-lasting aspects of your personality. Unless you are an extraordinary leader in a very senior leadership role, you are also unlikely to be able change the basic culture of the organisation you are thinking of joining.

Other examples would be that if in your working life to date you have placed a very strong emphasis on the personal development of the individual members of your team, if you have a passionate belief in sustainability in environmental terms, or if you have always been very concerned about long-term community relationships – it would be unlikely to be a good idea for you to work for an organisation (perhaps a private equity owned company) whose values were more along the lines of:

> 'I need to know how much money you can make for me, at how little cost and at how little risk. I like you today, but you had better ask me tomorrow. If you

are interested in personal or team development, community relations and the environment, that is fine – but it is of no interest to me.'

In a company like this there may well be a clash between your longer-term and broader concerns and the more tightly financially focused values of your employer. This would therefore be a high-risk appointment for you because you would be unlikely to be able to change the underlying organisational culture and you would also be unlikely, or unwilling, to be able to change those basic aspects of your personality of which you are most proud. Such an appointment may therefore be likely to end in failure for you.

Therefore, the key point here is to *be aware* of your **Feelings** on key issues and to try and find an environment where your feelings on these key issues will be likely to be similar to those of the organisation who employs you. Even if you can't easily explain or understand your feelings in certain circumstances, they are a good indication that whatever caused them is important to you and therefore it would be high-risk to ignore them.

Inner World – can influence – "Thinking"

However, in some cases you may be able to influence the inner world of both your ideas and those of your potential employer. You may be able to develop a new business model or way of thinking about a problem or opportunity and hence influence how your potential employer addresses an important issue. You may be more up to date in your thinking, or able to use insights from a previous role or different sector in a way that is attractive and relevant to them and make you much more attractive as someone they may consider hiring.

The types of issues that you will think about in this quadrant are:

- Your skills and abilities. What are the key skills you have developed and how might they be useful to your target organisations? Do you need to learn new ones? If so, how will you go about this?
- Think about your attitudes on issues that may be relevant to your future working life. Do you have views that might put off a potential employer? Do you tend to be more negative than positive in conversations? How would you like to present yourself at interview? On the whole, most people prefer a constructive, positive approach and enthusiasm.

Being well prepared, thoughtful and able to present your case persuasively and succinctly is important here. This will distinguish you from your potential competitors and may be an area that excites both your and their interests.

The key word here is "**Thinking**"

Boundary issues

In the boundary between the inner world, which is hard to influence, and the world that you *can* influence, at least to some degree, lie issues such as your motivation and values.

As with most things in life, motivation is critical to success in attaining your preferred working future.

The Snooker Tournament: motivation

Some years ago, I used to play snooker most Friday nights with my friends as an enjoyable form of relaxation. Imagine the scene where I am entering the snooker club on a Friday night in November and there is a notice on the board about a snooker tournament that will be held in April.

Now consider two scenarios:

Scenario 1

As I look at the poster advertising the snooker tournament I think:

- I would really like to win that tournament, that would be great.
- I am a good snooker player, but not a great one.
- There are lots of really good, and maybe even great, snooker players in this club.
- If I was to win this tournament, I would have to practise a lot to have a chance of winning.
- But most of the players I would be practising with are a lot better than me and so I would lose most of the matches I play.
- Thinking about it a bit more, I would not enjoy being beaten by them regularly.
- And so, on reflection, I will not bother entering the tournament.

Scenario 2

Scenario 2 is identical to Scenario 1 – with the exception of your attitude:

- I would really like to win that tournament, that would be great – I can imagine myself holding up the cup in front of my friends.
- I am a good snooker player but not a great one.
- There are lots of really good and maybe even great snooker players in this club.
- If I was to win this tournament, I would have to practise a lot to have a chance of winning.
- But most of the players here are a lot better than me.
- But I *really* would like to win that tournament.
- So I had better get started as soon as possible so I can get to play better and have a chance of winning.

The overall circumstances are identical in both scenarios and the only thing that is different is your attitude or motivation – having a positive mental attitude, as in the second scenario, may greatly affect the outcome. The point about Scenario 1 is that there is only one possible outcome – you won't win the tournament, because you have decided you won't enter it.

The outcome in Scenario 2 is uncertain – you may win, or you may not win – but you have a chance of winning because you are prepared to put a considerable amount of effort into increasing your chances of success, even though you are realistic enough to realise that it will be a tough challenge.

Your *motivation* is therefore critical, and this is something that you can influence to at least some degree by focusing hard upon what success would mean to you and what you have to do to increase your chances of success.

You may well also find that regular exercise in a form you enjoy helps you deal with some of the stress of not knowing what your next job will be and help you be more positive in your overall frame of mind.

Values

Your personal values are important – to some individuals they are very important indeed. If, for example, high standards of integrity, personal conduct and financial probity have always been important to you in your working life to date, this is an important consideration in your choice for your working future.

If, on the other hand, you are most conscious of your financial imperatives – you have a mortgage to pay and young children who you want to make sure are properly educated and you mainly consider yourself as a "hired gun" then the underlying values of the organisation you work for may be less important to you in these circumstances.

In any case, it is a good idea that you reflect on what your core values are – that have determined how you actually behaved on issues that are really important to you – and that you allow these to influence the choice of the next part of your working life. You may be prepared to make some trade-offs or compromises, or there may be issues that you know you would never be able to compromise because you could not live with yourself afterwards.

It is therefore sensible for you to consider what your values are and to what degree, if any, you would be willing to make trade-offs. You should do what you can to reduce the risk of a poor fit between your values and those of your potential employer by doing such things as:

- trying to find current or ex-employees (e.g. via LinkedIn) and seeing what it is really like to work there
- checking out all recent public statements from the company
- talking to anyone in your contacts who may know someone who works or used to work there
- checking websites such as Glassdoor to see what employees think.

In this sense, you need to consider both what you **think** and what you **feel.**

Outer world – can influence: "Doing"

A few years ago, I was working with a client who had, until recently, been chief executive of a financial services company. I was helping him prepare for an important interview by role playing. After about ten minutes of this he said:

"Mike, I am really not very happy about this." (He had a dry sense of humour.) "In fact, I am thinking of making a complaint."

"Oh really. I am sorry to hear that," I said. "What is the problem?"

"I am not in control."

As a former chief executive, he was very much used to being in control of most things. He was used to interviewing candidates, not being interviewed, and was finding it very difficult to be relatively passive.

"I see," I said. "No, you are not in control. In a few weeks you may be being interviewed by someone who is twenty years younger than you, and in the next hour, what they decide may well determine the next five years of your working life. You are not in control of that at all. But what you are in control of is how you prepare for that interview, what research you do, how you dress for it, how you tell your story and what questions you ask. You are largely in control of those issues, and I suggest that is what we should focus on, because how you prepare may well make the difference between whether you get offered that job or not."

He went on to be offered a role that he was very well suited to and described the coaching support that he had received in the process as his "secret weapon".

When you have become aware of relevant external trends, have considered how you feel about key issues affecting your working future, and devoted some thought to how you could influence your target organisation with some original thinking, it is time to move into **"Doing"** mode – those areas of your future that are both external and about which you can bring about change.

- Does your CV look professional and is it persuasive about why they should choose you? Can an employer find the key information about you as a candidate in the first few seconds of reading it? Is it no more than three pages long? (I will give more detailed advice on the preparation of your CV in Chapter 8.)

- Have you spoken to everyone you know well in your network and told them what sort of role you are looking for? (See Chapter 9.)

- What knowledge do you have about the type of roles you are most interested in? Do you have examples that demonstrate you will work well in these roles? Do you know what best practice is in this area? Can you provide examples from your working life to date that demonstrate you have been able to apply best practice and gain the benefits from successful implementation of these best practices? Is your technical knowledge in your area of specialisation up to date? Do you need to do something about this?

- How much research have you done about the organisation that is considering employing you? Have you checked the background of those interviewing you?

- How will you dress for the interview? Have you checked the LinkedIn profiles of senior executives? Do they dress formally or informally? You will want to seem as if you belong to the organisation and not dress in a way that shows you are not "one of us".

- Have you thought of the main questions that you might be asked at interview, e.g. why did you leave your last employer? Why are you a uniquely strong candidate for this role and can you explain why this is the case? (More on this in Chapter 12.)

- Have you spoken to everyone you know who might be able to give you insights into what it might be like to work for this organisation?
- What state of physical health are you in? Do you exercise regularly in a way that you enjoy? Are there health risks that you could manage more effectively? Do you have the energy necessary for a demanding new role? Is staying as healthy as you reasonably can be a routine and important part of your life?
- Are you well-prepared for a video call? Does the background look appropriate? Are you fairly sure you won't be interrupted? Is your face well-lit so you are not in silhouette?

The key word in this quadrant is "**Doing**". An adage I like in this context is that attributed to Gary Player: "The harder I work, the luckier I get." (Also attributed variously to Coleman Cox and Thomas Jefferson.) You should focus hard on the preparation you can do and do it thoroughly and effectively.

Using a more planned approach to reduce the risk of regret later in life

We are each responsible for trying to create a working future for ourselves that will meet the immediate needs of ourselves and our families (if we have one). We only have one life, and one working life, and if we think forward to the point at which we were approaching the end of our lives, it would be very sensible for us to have thought about how we could reduce the likelihood that we would have serious regrets about the working life we have led, since it will be too late, at that point, to do anything about it. David Cooper (2010) points out that research conducted with people close to the end of their lives shows that amongst the most common regrets are: "I wish I had had more fun; I wish I had taken more risks; I wish I had told the people who really matter to me that they really did matter to me". Whether we realise it or not and whether we do anything about it or not, each of us has important choices at different points in our working lives that will take us towards different futures – some of which will be better or worse for us.

Many of my clients say that in their lives to date, they have never really considered what they want to gain from their working lives other than to pay their mortgage. They have often moved from one job to another without too much reflection. Maybe they have been tapped on the shoulder by a senior colleague and asked to perform a new role. I generally encourage my clients to understand that many of them are now at a point in their lives where they can think of all the different things they might be able to do, choose the one that they are most excited by – and which there is evidence that they would be good at – and then I work with them so that we can create their preferred future together. They can think of this as an adventure, which it usually is. This does not mean that it is easy – it usually isn't!

Because technology is bringing about significant changes in the world of work, because unforeseen events can also bring about significant changes and because you will evolve and develop in terms of your own experience and motivations, I suggest it is unlikely to be useful to try and plan in detail much more than five years ahead, arguably even as short as eighteen months.

Combining the opportunistic and planned approaches

It is obviously true that the external factors in life (e.g. economic policy, international politics) and the changing nature of working lives (e.g. driven by technology) are difficult to predict and so agility and an ability to be opportunistic are important. If, however, you do understand very well what you are best at, and you are very well-prepared (as above) for opportunities that arise, you may well be able to have the best of both worlds: to plan to be able to take best advantage of any appropriate opportunities that do arise and also to proactively find opportunities to which you would be very well-suited. You will greatly increase the likelihood of your success if you prepare very carefully on those subjects in the quadrant of the outer world for which you can prepare – the world of action.

It is also possible that the most appropriate approach may change over the course of your working life, particularly if you have a large mortgage or young children, you may have to be relatively opportunistic, after all, you do need a job and you probably need it soon. As you get closer to the end of your active working life, and have hopefully paid off your mortgage and your children are financially independent, you might have more scope to decide what you really want to do – you can take a more planned approach to working out what activity or range of activities you would most enjoy – and so you can adopt a more carefully planned approach to your future working life.

Conclusions

1. An opportunistic approach is possible, and you should be prepared to react to opportunities that arise, which you have not really planned for. If you have a short and very clear Mission Statement (Chapter 7) this will help you evaluate unforeseen opportunities.

2. The world of work is changing, and will continue to change rapidly, and so the notion of a long-term career is probably not going to be very helpful. Arguably, you should not try to plan much more than five years ahead of your working life, maybe even just plan for the next eighteen months.

3. Using David Cooper's four quadrant model – the inner and outer world and what you can change and what you cannot change – should be very helpful in the development of an appropriate plan for you.

4. In your preparation, once you have decided what sort of role you will be well-suited to, most of your time will be spent on preparing for those practical issues, such as your CV, interview preparation and personal networking, over which you can have quite a lot of influence. It will not be very helpful worrying about issues where you have little or no control, although you do need to be aware of them.

5. Reflecting on what your values are and whether they seem to fit the organisations you are targeting is very important. If there is not a reasonable match between your values and those of your employer, you are much more likely to fail in your role, and so your due diligence on these issues is important.

6. Your personal motivation is also very important. Interviewers will quickly pick up if you are enthusiastic about the role being discussed. If you are not too enthusiastic at the beginning of your new role, how likely are you to lose motivation when problems begin to emerge, as they inevitably will?
7. Paying attention to broader issues, such as your health and finding a form of exercise that you can enjoy regularly, will also be likely to help your overall frame of mind and therefore how likely you are to succeed.
8. What may work best for most people is to prepare and plan carefully on those issues that you can largely control and go looking proactively for the opportunities that you are best suited to. Your careful preparation will also be very likely to help you perform well when unforeseen opportunities arise, which you can respond to in a reactive way.

Chapter 5

Taking a Longer-Term View
Consciously Developing Your Life Vision

Sometimes it can be helpful *not* to focus directly on what you would like your next job to be but rather to take a few steps back and consider how you would like your life to be in several years' time. If you develop a clear picture of how you would like your life to be at some time in the future, you can then work backwards from it and as you find particular opportunities to consider, you can decide if this possibility would take you towards or away from your "Life Vision". You can then decide whether it would be a good step for you to take.

Having a clear picture of your medium-term preferred future life can therefore be helpful. Some people do find the exercise below useful and others less so. You can see if it works well for you.

Of course, the vision of how you would like your life to be needs to be something that you could have a reasonable chance of achieving, e.g. that you could manage financially given the route you are exploring.

If you do answer these questions thoughtfully, and follow them up with appropriate actions and choices, you are more likely to be happier, healthier and more effective in what you do.

You could, therefore, consider (possibly with your partner) your answers to these questions as an exercise to help you gain a clearer view of what sort of medium-term future you would prefer.

1. A happier life

a. Picturing yourself three to five years from now, how will you (and your partner) know you have both been leading a mainly happy life?

....

....

....

....

....

b. Considering the things that have *actually* given you the most satisfaction in the last few years, what does this suggest about what might give you considerable satisfaction in the next five years or so? In what ways might this be changing?

....

....

....

....

....

c. Imagining yourself three or five years into your preferred future, what sort of things would you most like to have achieved?

....

....

....

....

....

d. How would you have liked to have spent most of your time?

....

....

....

....

....

2. **An ideal job for you**

a. Is there a type of job or organisation that has a real *purpose* that you feel passionate about and which would bring a greater sense of meaning to your life?

....

....

....

....

....

b. Would you need new skills that would allow you to move towards such a job/organisation? How could you acquire them?

....

....

....

....

....

c. In what ways can you constructively use your existing friends and contacts to help you gain such a role? Most people are happy to be asked for their advice.

....

....

....

....

....

3. **One role or more than one role?**

a. It could be that you would like one role or that you decide that you would prefer to have more than one role (e.g. working as a commercial consultant and working in a charity). This is an important decision to take. You might like to look for several different, interesting ways of spending your time, or earning money from several part-time sources.

....

....

....

....

....

This portfolio approach is likely to take longer to develop and achieve, but it is flexible and will provide variety, and possibly, a higher degree of resilience.

b. Will this portfolio of activities leave you enough time to spend with your friends and family and take a form of exercise you enjoy?

....

....

....

....

....

c. Would having several different activities allow you to feel more in control of your life because you are not dependent on a single organisation?

....

....

....

....

....

4. Relationships

a. What relationships (personal, professional or community) is it important you invest in over the next few years?

....

....

....

....

....

b. What steps will you take to spend the time and effort on them that is required?

....

....

....

....

....

c. Does this mean you will need to alter the trade-offs you have been making? (e.g. in your work-life balance.)

....

....

....

....

....

d. What sort of people would you like to have been spending more time with – and what sort less?

....

....

....

....

....

5 Your Focus

a. Your time and energy are limited – where is it most important that you focus them to give you the most personal fulfilment?

....

....

....

....

....

b. What will you be most pleased that you have been doing less of?

....

....

....

....

....

c. What do you intend to spend more time thinking about, and what less, so that you can pay attention to what *actually makes you happy* rather than worry about things you can't change?

6. External Factors

a. Are there critical external factors that must be taken into account? (e.g. ageing parents, location of family, health risks, stress.)

....

....

....

....

....

b. Where do you hope to be living? Are there alternatives?

....

....

....

....

....

c. Could you reduce your commuting time and the extent to which you are "always on" as far as your work is concerned?

....

....

....

....

....

7. **Money**

a. What would you like your financial situation to be like? How feasible is this?

....

....

....

....

....

b. Are there financial imperatives that must be met? How will you most likely be able to meet them?

....

....

....

....

....

c. Are there any ways in which you might be able to worry less about money, e.g. by better budgeting and control? (High levels of debt are more associated with depression than low levels of income.)

....

....

....

....

....

d. Are there trade-offs between what you would *like* to be the case financially and other issues that will be very important to your well-being? (e.g. health, time with family, pursuing unpaid interests). How will you make these choices consciously?

....

....

....

....

....

7. Unpaid activities

a. Are there unpaid activities (e.g. charity work, volunteering, your favourite hobby) that would give you satisfaction and where you have useful skills?

....

....

....

....

....

b. How could you work your way to doing more of these?

....

....

....

....

....

8. **Building commitment**

a. Looking backwards from your vantage point in the future, what has made you most proud in the last few years?

....

....

....

....

....

b. If you go a long way to achieving this vision, how do you think it will feel for (both of) you?

....

....

....

....

....

c. Things will change unpredictably in your life in the next few years, and some risks may not be avoidable, but are you ready to make a deal with yourself (and your partner) that this is where you would like to be going? What is the deal?

....

....

....

....

....

d. Is there something you will do *today* that will start you on this journey?

....

....

....

....

....

If you have answered these thoughtfully and honestly then you will now have an overall sense of direction that you wish to follow in your life and are therefore much more likely to get there! You will also have a framework within which you can make individual decisions.

It will probably be helpful to write down your answers and look at them a few days later and see if the picture you have painted of your life excites you. Remember, it is a good tip to *follow what gives you energy.*

It is also a good idea to have another look at your answers in a few years' time, as what is important to you may change over time, and you should recognise this.

Chapter 6

Flexible Working

In addition to the effects on our physical and mental health, the COVID-19 Pandemic has had a profound, and very likely, long-lasting effect on the pattern of very many of our working lives. I strongly suspect that one of the unforeseen aftereffects of the pandemic will be one of the biggest and fastest changes in the way we work, where we work, and the way we think about work since the Industrial Revolution in the nineteenth century. The optimist in me thinks that this might be very liberating for many individuals and more enlightened organisations.

The effect on us as individuals will vary depending on our particular circumstances. If your work is physical, or cannot be done remotely, or if you have young children to look after that makes homeworking more difficult, your experience will be very different from a case where it is relatively easy to do your work online.

If you have any tendency towards depression or anxiety, this may well make periods of isolation from friends and family particularly difficult.

When, after not being able to see my children and grandchildren for a year during the pandemic we were finally able to get together, my three-year-old granddaughter did not run towards her grandmother for her usual hug but clung to her mum, saying that she felt "nervous". It occurred to me that for about one third of her life she had been warned by her parents that she must avoid any physical contact with others. Although she seemed to recover from this nervousness quite quickly, I wondered what the medium- and longer-term impact of this feeling would be.

For many of us, the pandemic provided an opportunity to seriously reconsider what is really important in our lives. Some of us may have come to the conclusion that buying the latest gadget or fashionable piece of clothing is less important than being able to spend time freely with those we love. Many of us have learnt we enjoy being free from daily commuting and are very unlikely to return to it.

In very many cases, the way we think about our work and how we do it will have changed substantially as a result of the pandemic, and the purpose of this chapter is to help us think about the issues around flexible working as it relates to us, the work we do and our preferred employers.

Work: technology enablement and location dependency

We can therefore give some more thought to the sort of changes that the pandemic has brought about and how we might like to change the way we prefer to work as a consequence. The changes that are happening appear to be giving individuals, at least at present, more flexibility than they may have had historically.

It is likely that many of us will be finding an appropriate place for ourselves on a spectrum, one end of which is where we need to be physically present or co-located for the work to be done (e.g. building work, hands-on care of the elderly, childcare, refuse collection) with being a real digital nomad at the other end of the spectrum, where any link between physical location and work has been almost entirely dissolved. Many of us will be settling somewhere towards the middle of the spectrum, where we can deliver our service either face to face or remotely. Many professional services will be around this mid-point.

Ideally, we will be able to choose where is the most appropriate place and time to do our work – at home, in the office, in a space of co-workers, in the coffee shop or on the train. This is *flexible working*, on which I hope many organisations will trust their employees to make their own decisions, within a broad policy framework.

In all cases of flexible or hybrid working, or cases where work can be provided independently of location, technology, mainly the internet, will play an essential role in enabling the service to be provided remotely.

To give us an idea of how these two dimensions (technological enablement and location dependency) might work we can consider several examples as in the figure below. The figure is conceptual, and a case could be made for choosing somewhat differing locations on the matrix for the different types of work, but the main point of the illustration is that *one size does not fit all types of work.*

The Relationship between Technological Enablement and Location Dependency with Different Types of Work

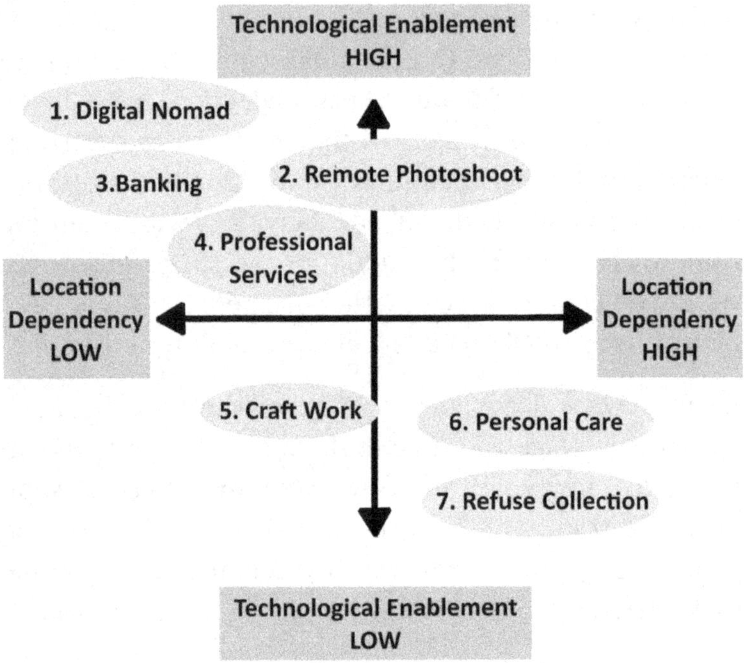

1. Digital Nomad

Here the need for technological enablement is high as this type of work would clearly be impossible without digital technology, whilst the location dependency is very low since the digital nomad (see page 138) can do their work anywhere on earth, with the need only to manage time zones.

2. Photoshoots

In the case of a photoshoot (see page 141) the need for technological enablement will be high if the photoshoot is virtual or remote, but photoshoots can also be conducted on a co-located basis, and so the location dependency is medium but moving towards low in this new business model.

3. Banking

In traditional high street banking, the location dependency was high but in recent years this has dramatically reduced with internet banking. The pandemic has arguably accelerated this trend. This is another example where the positioning on this matrix is quite dynamic, not static.

4. Professional Services

Before the pandemic, many professional services were co-located with delivery. Now, very many professional services, e.g. the career transition support work I do (see page 143), can be delivered remotely. The pandemic has also significantly increased change in the way professional services can be delivered.

5. Craft Work

Craft work historically was very local and the actual work of craft production still clearly is. On the other hand, the sales, marketing and distribution of craft products can now be conducted independently of the location of production via the internet.

6. Personal Care

Although some aspects of personal care will be technology enabled (e.g. work scheduling) the actual delivery of personal care has, of course, to be physically co-located, with the caregiver and the person being cared for in the same place.

7. Refuse Collection

Although management of the refuse collection service may be provided to a degree remotely, the actual collection of refuse has to be conducted where the refuse is physically located (page 140).

What we have learnt about Technological Enablement and location dependency

Even this simple consideration of these examples demonstrates two principles:

1. One size definitely does not fit all. (This idea is supported by Boston College et al, 2023, see below). How independent of location the work can be conducted varies significantly with the work being done.
2. The degree of location dependency can change quite quickly. Very many roles that have traditionally been conducted locally have rapidly moved online where they can be conducted quite effectively.

Some real-life examples

A virtual services business: the story of a digital nomad – Saloua Ibaline

Saloua comes from a small village in Morocco. After her parents' divorce, Saloua and her mother immigrated to Belgium where she grew up and studied. Saloua benefited from three "angels" in her life:

- In Belgium, her part-time foster family introduced her to things she might otherwise never have experienced (theatre, museums, horseback riding) and helped her with her homework.
- At the age of twenty-one, Saloua moved to New York City alone, with neither money nor connections. She worked her way up from nothing and eventually landed a job at an upscale restaurant where she met a fellow immigrant woman from Cuba who offered her help when she was in distress.
- A strong, powerful woman, her former boss from the restaurant, who ran several businesses, agreed to be her sponsor.

With the determined spirit of her mother, and knowing that she wanted to become an entrepreneur, Saloua eventually set up a successful global coaching business and in 2021 wrote a book, *The Stories of Immigrant Women Entrepreneurs in the United States of America*, with the hope that it would be a catalyst for change in our views and opinions about immigrants, especially immigrant women who had dared to leave everything behind to follow their entrepreneurial dreams in the USA.

In 2019 she set off to be a digital nomad, with no permanent geographic base, and travelled to over twenty-eight countries on three continents over three years, working from anywhere. What she learnt from the experience was:

1. **How to live a minimalist lifestyle:** letting go of stuff is not easy, having only her carry-on luggage and backpack.

2. **Don't believe the hype on social media**: the life of a digital nomad is not easy and not for everyone, particularly with no financial support. You need to be good at finding ways of making money and be extremely good at budgeting.
3. **Uncertainty will rule your day**: she was not able to do any of the things she had planned, particularly with the onset of the pandemic and lockdown requirements.
4. **Self-awareness is very important**: as a digital nomad you are your own best friend and worst enemy and so you have to be very self-aware. You also have to understand that it will not be possible to build deep relationships in this lifestyle.
5. **You will need to find balance and stay grounded**: to make this work you will need to be very self-disciplined (e.g. working regular hours) and develop and follow a strict routine.

Saloua's story shows how, at one end of the spectrum, it is possible to almost completely break the relationship between physical location and work – but there are significant pros and cons to this lifestyle.

Refuse collection – moderate change and a flexible policy: Greener Ealing Ltd.

Greener Ealing Ltd. is mainly a refuse collection business with its origins in local government. During the pandemic it had various challenges to contend with, such as a shortage of HGV drivers, but the refuse still had to be collected. Many customers expressed their gratitude for these front-line workers continuing to do their job at some risk to their health at the time.

The main changes that were implemented were:

- The front-line operations underwent relatively little change, but the management and support functions moved online, at least to a limited degree.
- A flexible working policy was developed with individual and personal circumstances being taken into account, e.g. a young apprentice was allowed to work in the office five days per week since she had no separate physical space from which to work at home and wanted to learn from physical involvement in operations and to enjoy informal and social contact with colleagues.
- The finance function could, on the other hand, do most of its work remotely.
- For many of the supporting services, a rota was developed whereby preference was given to working in the office on specified days each week. The purpose of this arrangement was to ensure that when employees did work in the office, their colleagues would be more likely to also be physically present on the same day so they could have the benefit of informal interaction.

How specialist technology allowed a new business model: virtual photoshoots – Joanne Moorhouse

After her first job as a library assistant, many years ago, Joanne has helped hundreds of professionals get their message across with authentic photographs that reflect their brand. With the first lockdown in 2020 she had to devise a new business model. Using specialist photographic apps (Clos and Shutter) she became an early adopter of the technology as a virtual photoshoot manager. Using the apps, she now sends clients a secure link that allows her to use her client's phone to take photographs in a virtual photoshoot. Her client (or a friend of her client) holds the phone, props it up in the right place, or uses a tripod, while Joanne takes the photographs, then edits them and sends them back to her client via the Cloud.

The advantages are:

- As a photographer she can now operate anywhere in the world remotely, and is writing a book, *Remote Stories Around the World*, with all of the photographs being taken remotely.
- The remote photoshoot is much more flexible and time-efficient with no need to travel.
- The quality of the images is now very good – as good as the phone being used.
- This style of photoshoot works very well for clients who may otherwise be intimidated by the appearance of a professional photographer with lots of specialist equipment. This style of remote photoshoot is likely to put clients at ease much more quickly.
- The photos can be edited remotely e.g., to give a common visual background.

- With a much-reduced carbon footprint (no travel) it is much more environmentally friendly.
- There are serious cost savings.

Providing support during career transition: my own case

Like all my career transition self-employed colleagues, I was able to move my work online within a couple of days of the pandemic restrictions. Advising clients during the period of their career transition is an activity that works pretty well online. Previously, I had commuted weekly from Glasgow to London to have meetings at our office, with only a small percentage of meetings online. Within a few days, very nearly all my meetings were online. Interestingly, I found that the average meeting time reduced from about ninety minutes to about sixty minutes. I think this was because online meetings tend to be inherently more transactional – less time talking about, "how was your trip", getting a cup of coffee, etc. On the other hand, I certainly miss the informal chat with colleagues and having some discussions over lunch or dinner. Towards the end of the pandemic, when I started a one-week-per-month pattern of travelling from Glasgow to London to physically attend a board meeting (instead of my previous weekly commute) I found:

- In the pre-dinner discussions with my board colleagues, I had to re-find the skills of small talk, which I had to a fair extent forgotten during the pandemic.
- When I finally looked for a suit to wear, I discovered it had been eaten by moths.

- In choosing face-to-face meetings I found myself more consciously choosing who I did actually want to spend face-to-face time with.

How COVID-19 has fundamentally changed the nature of work for many: key questions

There is very little doubt that the COVID-19 Pandemic has in practical terms changed the nature of work quite profoundly for a large percentage of the population and leaves us with some questions to which it will take a while to find answers to:

Questions for employers:

- What will be the effect on productivity and creativity of an increased number of employees working from home? (I mean productivity in the broader sense of adding value rather than the narrow sense of conducting a given process more efficiently.) As below, we already have (self-reported) indications that the large majority of individuals working from home believe they can get at least as much done working from home as in an office. There is also some evidence that a four-day week can increase productivity.
- Is there a sweet spot where businesses can reduce real estate costs and employees can also be more in control of their working lives whilst being at least as productive as previously with less time spent on unproductive and stressful commuting? How should these financial benefits be shared?

- What are the motivational, legal, contractual, technical, security, environmental and financial implications of flexible ways of working? What is an employer's duty of care for employees when they are working from home?
- What are the implications of a flexible pattern of working for leadership and supervisory roles?
- What are the implications for support roles and functions?
- How do we sensibly negotiate our way through this so that we will be an attractive and successful employer that will attract and retain talent?
- What should our revised policies be? To what extent will they be mandatory or flexible to individuals' circumstances?

Questions for you as an employee:

- How did my employer react to the requirements of the pandemic in the treatment of their employees? Empathetically or brutally? How do I feel about the way they reacted?
- Is my employer talking about changing the terms and conditions of my contract and am I happy about them? What are the overall financial implications for me?
- Have I changed my views about what really matters to me in my working life? Am I re-balancing my priorities in terms of issues such as work-life

balance, commuting, being in the office, the importance of the social aspects of work?

- Do I want to consider changing my employer or the place and type of work I am happy to do after this experience?
- Now I value the experience of spending more time with my family and increased flexibility, has this changed my expected retirement date?
- Should I be thinking about becoming self-employed?
- With the experience of working during the pandemic (assuming this was possible for you) what have you learnt about how you would *prefer to* work in future?

Findings from recent research on flexible working

From recent research, what do we know so far?

Before 2020, it had taken almost forty years for homeworking to grow by three percentage points, but its prevalence grew eight-fold virtually overnight as people were instructed to work at home, if they could, because of the pandemic. Despite theories and predictions to the contrary, employees reported that their productivity was not adversely affected. Seven out of ten employees said that they were able to get as much done while working at home in June 2020 as they were able to do six months earlier. By September 2020, this proportion had risen to 85%. (Felstead and Reuschke, 2021). There is an important qualification here: this research considers *self-*

reported productivity. Whether their organisations have *actually* experienced better, or at least no worse, levels of productivity with increased home working is less clear. It is also less clear whether there has been an economically visible increase in productivity.

From a survey conducted by YouGov for Deloittes in 2021 almost three-quarters (70%) of employees working in financial services rated their working from home experience as positive:

- Not having to commute was considered the top reason for a positive experience.
- More than three-quarters felt they were as or more productive working from home during the lockdown.
- The number of people expect to work from home more than twice a week tripled post-lockdown.
- When asked what makes the experience positive, more than three-quarters (76%) cited not having to commute as the top reason. This was followed by having more flexibility (43%), being able to spend more time with the family (39%) and having more time to exercise (28%).
- Employee well-being has also taken a positive turn with more than a third (36%) stating their well-being had improved during lockdown, against just under a quarter (24%) who said it has worsened.

In a different survey, nearly one-third (28.1%) of respondents reported that they had felt lonely or isolated (36) when homeworking.

In an authoritative and substantial piece of survey research (Government Property Agency, 2020) *Homeworking and the UK Civil Service, Leesman Homeworking Survey*, with 25,290 respondents in July 2020 some of the interesting findings were:

- In general, homes were on average supporting employees better than the average office.
- Just 27% of respondents indicated a preference to return to the office for the majority of the working week once COVID-19 restrictions were removed.
- Only 66.7% of Civil Service employees felt connected to their colleagues and 69.3% felt connected to the organisation when working from home, suggesting that the social dimensions of work life are not consistently supported at home.
- Employee well-being can also be at risk, with 72.7% of Civil Service employees stating that they are able to maintain a healthy work-life balance when working from home, leaving more than one in four (27.3%) struggling.
- The 39% of respondents who stated they worked from a dedicated work room or office reported the best home working experience, whilst the 35% who used a non-work specific area (such as a dining table) reported the worst. These findings suggest that employees who do not have a room at home they can dedicate for working are more likely to experience challenges in doing both individual and collaborative work, maintaining a healthy work-life balance and ensuring appropriate ergonomics.

Flexible working is popular but what about productivity?

As I mentioned above, the initial findings about flexible working and *self-reported* productivity are encouraging but *The Results are In: The UK Four Day Week Pilot,* (the joint product of research teams at Boston College, the University of Cambridge and Autonomy Research Ltd., 2023) gives more encouraging evidence that a carefully tailored approach to flexible working may *increase* productivity. The report details the full findings of the world's largest four-day working week trial to date, comprising 61 companies and 2,900 workers that took place in 2022:

- "Of the 61 companies that participated, 56 are continuing with the four-day week (92%), with 18 confirming the policy is a permanent change." (Boston College, 2023.)
- "Other key business metrics also showed signs of positive effects from shorter working hours. Companies' revenue, for instance, stayed broadly the same over the trial period, rising by 1.4% on average, weighted by company size, across respondent organisations. When compared to a similar period from previous years, organisations reported revenue increases of 35% on average, which indicates healthy growth during this period of working time reduction." (Boston College, 2023.)

Tentative conclusions from research so far

It is too early to reliably conclude what the effects on working patterns will be following the global pandemic, but we can probably draw some tentative conclusions:

- The effect on our daily working patterns has been, and will be, profound and it seems likely that there will be in many cases long-lasting changes in the way we work compared to pre-pandemic patterns of working.
- Although up to 85% of individuals feel that they are at least as productive working from home as in the office, most of this early research is self-reported.
- From the largest trial of a four-day week to date, 56 of the 61 (91%) participating companies intend to continue with the four-day week and during the four-day week trial average revenues increased by 35% compared with a similar period from previous years.
- For many, working from home has been a positive experience but almost one-third of respondents reported that they felt lonely during periods of homeworking or enforced isolation.
- Those civil servants with the best experience of home working are likely to have a dedicated working area and those with the worst are likely not able to have a dedicated home working space.
- Well-being of some employees can also be at risk, with 72.7% of Civil Service employees stating

that they are able to maintain a healthy work-life balance when working from home, leaving more than one in four (27.3%) struggling.

It seems very likely that there will be quite a long period of debate and negotiation between employees and employers about changes to their working patterns. Some of these issues may change relatively quickly, for example:

- Around the time of the end of the pandemic, much was written about the "Great Retirement" where a significant number of employees had decided that they did not want to continue working, perhaps because they had re-evaluated what was really important in their lives. Not very long after, with soaring energy costs and rampant inflation, some of those individuals found that they simply had to return to employment out of economic necessity.
- With unemployment in the UK currently being very low and with significant labour and skill shortages, power seemed to have shifted in the direction of employees, with increasing levels of strikes so that wages could keep closer to levels of inflation. If there is an economic recession, we might expect power to shift back in the direction of employers.

These are both examples of issues of which we are not in control of as individuals so what we should be doing is being very much aware of them and plan our working lives accordingly (as per David Cooper's framework in Chap. 4, page 105).

How should we think about changes in the way you prefer to work post-pandemic?

Employers will have a host of issues to think about in reconfiguring the ways of working post-pandemic. These include costs, management control, how to foster a team spirit, training and how to best encourage creativity and collaboration in an online, and perhaps more transactional and fragmented, work environment. Importantly, they will have to consider how they can best retain their most capable employees who have changed the way they think about their work. They may gain some useful insights from Karen Lojeski's and Richard Reilly's useful book, *The Power of Virtual Distance*, 2020, which suggests how reducing "Virtual Distance" can improve motivation, trust, and profitability.

It is also early days in terms of assessing both the medium-term economic impact of changes in work arrangements post-pandemic and to also consider some of the softer and more difficult to measure issues such as a sense of team cohesion, informal knowledge sharing, creative idea generation that is often sparked by face-to-face interaction, or the importance of the social pleasure of working in the same place.

Sustainability

Another dimension to the way we are changing the way we work is the environmental dimension. This is likely to be both an important and a permanent consideration. There is no doubt at all that organisations, large and small, will have to work out ways of working that are more environmentally sustainable. Remote, home, or flexible working will certainly make a contribution to this as lower levels of commuting will tend to reduce the carbon footprint of working, but this will need to be measured in each case.

How to assess new ways of working: well-being

It is clear that consideration will need to be given to the individual circumstances of the work being done and that one size does not fit all. In considering your own preferred next role you will doubtless give some thought to the degree to which the type of work you do can be delivered remotely or flexibly.

It is also likely that you will want to consider what policies and practices are being adopted by your potential employer and how well these suit your personal circumstances. Employers who take an inflexible approach and attempt to insist on a blanket one-size-fits-all ("Get back to the office!") or compulsory approaches will be likely to struggle to attract and retain capable employees who have learnt to value the advantages of flexible working.

In approaching discussions with employers as individuals, I suggest that we can assess appropriate new and flexible ways of working by considering the same factors that are likely to increase our overall level of well-being, i.e. we select our way of preferred working (to the extent we are able to choose) by considering to what extent it will be likely to help us:

1. develop a relatively strong sense of **purpose**

2. invest in personal, community or work **relationships**
3. feel that we are in **control of our lives** to a reasonable degree
4. **live in the present** and not be too anxious about the future or regretful about the past
5. provide enough time for a form of **exercise** that we enjoy.

The most relevant criteria in thinking about this may well be numbers 2, 3, and 5. It may be that the changes in the way we work post-pandemic will be on balance positive for many of us from a well-being perspective. Overlaying this will be assessing the new ways of working from an environmental perspective and this will need to be measured.

The concept of Ikigai (Chapter 1) might provide a useful tool for individuals to think about and evaluate new ways of working – and, indeed, for their employers to design new ways of working that support a strong "psychological contract" with their employees. This may be helpful since it will help them respond to what is really important in their employees' lives, and to design new working models and policies that take this into account.

Capable employees, who do not like the way their employer has reacted to the post-pandemic period in terms of working arrangements, are quite likely to vote with their feet and look for a new employer, particularly while UK unemployment levels are low. Although, as above, this balance of power may shift back to employers during a recession.

We should also remember that the more engaged we are as employees, and the happier we are working on a day-to-day basis, the more we are likely to be more productive and our employers more profitable.

Chapter 7

Your Mission

Now is where you can begin to pull it all together. Having considered what you can learn from your past, what actually makes you happy and how you might create your own preferred working future, you will now boil all of this down to a two-sentence description of what you want to do next: your mission. You may also be taking into account post-pandemic working arrangements and how well they suit your circumstances. Writing your two-sentence mission is an apparently simple, but certainly crucial, step in your journey to getting to where you want to go in the next stage of your working life. This is because being so concise and clear makes it very easy for your friends, colleagues and recruiters to help you. This is also what will drive all your networking discussions (see Chap. 9).

Not too broad – or too narrow

Your mission statement should not be too broad (e.g. "I want to make a difference") that it doesn't really help the person you are talking to make practical choices. It also should not be so precise that there will be very few opportunities (e.g. "I want an engineering maintenance job in aerospace within ten miles of Glasgow").

No more than two options

It should not contain more than two options, e.g. "I am considering a full-time role in advertising; I could set myself up as a freelance consultant; I would like to do something where I am giving back; I feel passionately about environmental issues – and I have a life-long interest in music." All of these statements may be true, but they make things difficult for your listener. There is a real risk that they may be thinking: this person is all over the place. They don't really know what they want to do and so I don't see how I can help them.

You should therefore use all that you have learnt about yourself in the work you have done in previous chapters to be as clear and succinct as you can be about what you want to do next. This has the further advantage that if someone asks the follow-up question, Why do you want to do that?" you will be able to provide a very clear and persuasive answer, for example:

- I have thought carefully about what I have done best in my career to date, and I am therefore confident I would be good at this.
- I have thought about what has previously motivated me and I know I would be excited about working in this area.

- I have considered carefully what I most want to do in the next part of my working life and this is what I would most like to do and why I would most like to do it.

Missing out on opportunities?

One of the things some of my clients get a bit concerned about is that if they make this statement too narrow, they will be missing out on possible opportunities. Of course, in theory this could be true, but if an opportunity arises that is widely different from your carefully considered mission statement it is less likely that it is something you would be very good at or enjoy very much, so you would not really be missing out. If you were to do something very different from your mission statement it is quite likely that this would be a high-risk decision because you would be taking on a job that you know would not be what you really wanted to do, or that in your heart of hearts, you know you would be really good at. You would, in fact, be risking being in the worst of all possible worlds in another year or so; you would have taken a job, which was not what you really wanted to do, you started off with a quite low level of motivation, which would likely get even worse as soon as soon challenges arise, which they inevitably will, and so you may well find yourself back on the job market having failed at this job, which you did not enjoy. You would also have a very difficult story to tell to explain why you are looking for a job again so soon. Your self-confidence will also probably have been rather dented.

Geography

Before you start your job search you should have given careful consideration to geography – where you would like to work. The smaller the geographic area you are prepared to consider, the lower the number of potential jobs there will be. Of course, it is a serious decision to move far from where you are now living. I should know, having worked in the UK, France, New Zealand and Indonesia and so I have a very good idea of how important an issue where you are going to live and work is. These may include the impact on relationships with friends and family, possibly needing to learn a new language and understand a different culture as well as practical issues like considering your children's education, not wanting to be too far away from ageing parents or having to deal with significant immigration formalities.

On the other hand, having lived and worked in these different countries and cultures has made my working experience far richer and more varied, and as a consequence, I believe, made me a much more versatile manager. The fact that our children lived in several quite different cultures has also made them much more versatile, adaptable and tolerant about different ways of thinking about issues, which I think will likely help them in their own lives.

Of course, post-pandemic working arrangements may give you a higher degree of geographical flexibility than pre-pandemic.

You will need to have considered all such issues and come to a conclusion on them before you start a serious job search or networking campaign, or you will risk spreading your efforts too thinly, wasting recruiters' time or confusing your audience and hence reducing your chances of success.

Trying out your mission

When you have come up with a mission statement that you are happy with you should try it out on a few of the people who know you best. You can ask them how this sounds to them because they know you very well. How does it sound to you yourself? When you say it are you excited about the possibility of working in that role? Does it sound right to you?

After you have tried it on a few of your closest contacts you will be confident about using it with a wider range of colleagues or recruiters and you will give a very clear answer to, "So what are you looking for now?" You will be confident because you have thought through your answer carefully. For this reason, you will also be more persuasive in interviews.

Conclusions

1. Although, on the face of it, writing two sentences about what you want to do next in your working life does not sound very difficult, it is one of the most important things you will do in your job search. If you get it right you will be more likely to end up working in a role you enjoy, in which you will be effective, and your new employer is more likely to be pleased with their decision to appoint you.

2. This statement needs to be clear and succinct – not more than two sentences and with not more than two options – so that it makes it easy for people to help you get to where you want to go.
3. It needs to be not too broad, nor too narrow, but a realistic statement of what you want to do next that should leave you to be considered for a reasonable number of opportunities.
4. Before you use your mission statement widely, try it out on a few of your colleagues who know you well and see how it sounds to them – and also to you.

Chapter 8

How to Structure and Write Your CV

There are a wide range of opinions about CVs' appropriate structure and style. The suggestions I make below are based on having worked with several hundred individual clients and having helped them to achieve their desired role, including by helping them with their CVs. This structure and style have received positive comments from recruiters and the vast majority of my clients have achieved roles that they have desired and pursued.

What follows are suggestions about how to structure and write your CV, and on page 166 is a good template structure with detailed notes against each section. It could be that you will use a different presentational style, but you will need, in any case, to clearly present the key information on the first page so that it has a quick and positive impact.

Remember that your CV gives your potential employer the first reason to reject you. The CV you send needs to be carefully tailored to the specific opportunity you are applying for – and not just a re-hash of previous versions. You can't change the basic facts of your working life, but you are very likely to be rejected at this early stage if your CV is poor in its visual appeal, structure, clarity of language, grammar, spelling or length. This is something important that you are actually in control of.

Recruiters may have to review hundreds of CVs from applicants for a single role. Your CV has mere seconds to do its job, which is to get you through to the next stage – ideally a conversation with the recruiting organisation. The first page should therefore be a succinct and almost self-standing summary of your suitability for that specific role. In the middle of that page should be a list of the organisations you have worked for, your roles and dates of employment. Research shows that this is what recruiters look for first and you must make it very easy for them to see that detail. If they are interested, they will turn the page. If not, your CV will immediately go into the rejection pile.

The maximum length of your CV is three pages. After your first page summary, the following two pages should give details of your career achievements.

Especially when networking with friends and colleagues, it is usually better to be asked to provide your CV rather than offering it unsolicited.

I should say that the style of CV I am suggesting is mostly aimed at private sector organisations. It could be, for example in an academic context, that the style and structure of what is considered to be a good CV may be different and you will need to be aware of this and adapt accordingly.

One further thought: recruitment now, particularly early in the process, is sometimes assisted by sophisticated technology. If your CV does not contain the appropriate words (often found in the information provided to applicants), you may be rejected before a human being has even looked at it. Therefore, it is worth taking time to ensure that key words in the application information are reflected in your CV. Any intelligence you can gather in advance about how selection decisions are actually going to be made is going to be helpful.

Tips

1. Check your spelling and language very carefully and ask someone else to review it. Two spelling mistakes, or unclear language in a CV, may result in immediate rejection even if you are very well suited to the job.
2. Fine-tune your CV to demonstrate how your experience is close to the Required Experience section of the application pack, if there is one.
3. It is not appropriate to put your date of birth on your CV.
4. You should include your nationality, but if you are applying outside your native country, make it clear that your immigration status permits you to work there.

5. Throughout your CV, avoid using abbreviations that are not very widely understood.
6. The purpose of your CV is to enable you to have a conversation with a potential employer. It is not a comprehensive story of your working life.
7. Send your CV as a PDF, not a Word doc., as the format can be changed in an unhelpful way (e.g. if composed on a Mac and it is read on a PC).
8. You don't need to add at the end, "References will be supplied on request". Recruiters will assume this – and you are wasting valuable space.
9. Make sure that information on your CV is consistent with what is on you LinkedIn profile. They are not the same, but content consistency is important.

Over the page is a good generic structure for an effective CV with detailed following notes.

Optional
Photo
[1]

Michael A. Smith [2]
Street Address [3]
Mob.: xxxxxxxxx
Email: xxxxxxxxxxxxxxx

PROFILE [4]

- Company doctor in turnaround, growth and private equity.
- Experienced NED and chairman in listed and bank-owned companies.
- Main board director of Power Plc during privatisation and flotation, focused on change and growth.
- Directorships in UK, France, Germany, Australia and New Zealand.
- Now working with HR Consultant Plc as career transition consultant.
- Strong interest in work and well-being.

KEY CAREER ACHIEVEMENTS [5]

- Advised some 300 senior executive clients on how to successfully make a career transition.
- TEDx speaker on work and well-being.
- As company doctor, provided three companies in financial trouble with a future.
- Helped change a large electricity company into a competitive service business.
- Advised World Bank how to spend $300 million on training environmental management specialists.

CAREER SUMMARY [6]

HR Consultancy	Senior Consultant	2007–Present
Company Doctor	CEO	1999–2006
Conglomerate Plc. NZ	CEO	1994–97
Power Co Plc.	Director	1990–94
Industrial Conglomerate	General Manager	1982–89

EDUCATION, QUALIFICATIONS AND PERSONAL [7]

BA joint hons.	University College, Wales	1970–74
MBA	Manchester Business School	1980–82
Languages:	French (degree level), working Indonesian	
Married:	Four grown-up children	
Interests:	Family history, work and well-being, photography	

CAREER HISTORY [8]

HR Consultancy [9]	Senior Consultant	2007- Present

Main Achievements [10]

- Helped 300 individual clients in their career transition.
- Advised more that 50 start-up businesses.
- Delivered TEDx talk on work and well-being.
- Published *Your Work, Your Well-Being: how to get a job you will be good at and enjoy.*
- Adviser to several small companies.

Company Doctor	**CEO**	**1999–2006**

- Company was massively over-indebted, suffering catastrophic customer losses and two companies in Europe and the USA had never been integrated.

- Debt/equity swap negotiated with nine lending banks reducing debt by €160 million and pattern of customer losses turned into €25 million of new business wins.
- Company was sold for some 12 times its 2004 EBITDA.

Conglomerate PLC. NZ CEO 1994–97

- Developed generation projects in New Zealand, Canada and Australia.
- Acquired 37.5% of Electricity Ltd. and exited for profit of NZ$32 million.
- Acquired 25% and exclusive marketing rights of Turbine Inc. in Los Angeles. Paul Allen Group and Bill Gates were subsequent investors. The shareholding acquired in 1995 for US$5 million had a value of over US$370 million in 2000.
- Chaired Gas Corp. Ltd., a publicly listed company of which my employer owned 33% (NZ$1 billion assets, 400 employees, NZ$50 million profit).

EARLY CAREER: INDONESIA 1974–80

World Bank 1980

Mission Member seconded form Education Foundation to advise on means of developing technical and managerial expertise in Indonesia with resources in Asia, North America, and Europe, committing US$300 million.

Education Foundation 1977–80

Project Manager working in the office of the Indonesian Minister of State for Environmental Management to design, establish and operate a selection and placement unit for staff who would manage natural resource management problems for a population of 130 million.

Natural Gas Liquefaction Co. 1976–77
Technical Language Training Adviser in a start-up joint venture to establish a multibillion-dollar gas liquefaction project in North Sumatra.

Voluntary Service Overseas 1974–77
Taught English to university, engineering, medical and agricultural staff in Java.

Detailed Notes

1. **Photograph**

   Including a photograph in the top right corner is optional. If you do include one, it should be a recent headshot, of high quality and about the same level of formality as the organisation you are applying to. It should look friendly and professional – not as if it is from your Facebook profile. The background should also be neutral – or interesting and relevant.

2. **Name, font choice and font size**

   The first line should only be your name (i.e. don't include Curriculum Vitae or CV). Include qualification abbreviations if they are very relevant (e.g. accounting qualifications) but not BA/BSc. If you wish, add a link here to your profile on LinkedIn. Your LinkedIn profile will not be exactly the same as your CV, but it must be consistent with it.

   The font throughout should be clear and modern in appearance e.g., Tahoma, Ariel or Calibri. Times New Roman looks old-fashioned. Try size 14 for your name, 12 for headings and 10 for the rest. You can use some colour for main headings to make it visually more interesting but make sure that it is dark enough to print well.

3. **Address, mobile and email**

   It is normal to include your street address, mobile and email address in a smaller font so that a recruiter does not need to go looking for your contact details. Usually just list your mobile number rather than a landline because your landline may not be answered professionally, and exact messages may not be passed on promptly.

4. **Profile**

   Several bullet points that sum up who you are and what you could bring to the organisation you are interested in. The language here needs to be relatively factual and not boastful, e.g. "A highly accomplished and respected business leader". This may be true, but the recruiter is likely to feel that it is up to them to make these judgements. You should also avoid clichés, e.g. "A proven track record in .... You can, and probably should, fine-tune this section depending on the organisation and role you are being considered for. The last bullet point could be along the lines "Now looking for ..." because your CV may be separated from your covering letter in the recruitment process. You would not want lots of organisations approaching you for a full-time role when you are only interested in part-time roles. Specifying this on your CV could save a lot of everybody's time.

5. **Key career achievements**

   Five to seven bullet points of the main things you have achieved during your career. Quantify some of them where possible. Make them as relevant as possible to your application. This section can be headed Key Skills if you prefer, with relevant key or functional skills listed instead. Some people write their CVs in the third person (he, she). Personally, I find this over formal. I think some use of "I" is OK, or just miss out pronouns.

6. **Career summary**

   Research shows that what professional recruiters want to see first is the summary of your organisation-role-date in that sequence. Do not include months in your role dates as that clutters the presentation visually. This section should *always* be in the middle of the front page. Recruiters will look at it for several seconds only in the first instance (so would you if you had a stack of fifty or more CVs to review). If they are interested in this section, they may look at the following page(s) for details. They may decide whether to put you on the list of possible candidates on the basis of what they see here. This should be a purely factual summary. If you have had a long career, you can add Early Career as a section, which summarises the first years of your career to save space. Recruiters will mainly be interested in the last ten years of your career. This section needs to go back to the end of your formal education with no gaps in years.

7. **Education, qualifications and personal**

   Usually only include the highest qualifications, such as degrees (i.e. not high school qualifications), and professional qualifications with organisation-qualification-date format. The order, like your CV, should be reverse chronological so the highest qualifications are first. If you have relevant training, include it in summary form.

   Personal may include something like: Married with two children (Aged: X,X). You can add if you have a clean driving licence if you wish, or if it is important to the role. Specifying whether you are married or not may seem old-fashioned, but the age of dependent children may be relevant to your employment circumstances.

   Interests should be one line with a short list. This adds a bit of personal colour and could be something to talk about during the interview.

8. **Career history**

   The second and possibly third page gives the details of your organisations and achievements in each role. Three pages in total is OK, but it is the maximum length. Recruiters don't have time to look at anything longer than three pages. Perhaps try for five or so achievements in your two most recent roles (three will be fine in earlier roles). You have an option of including a section on responsibilities in each section before achievements.

9. **Organisation Description**

   Especially if your employer is not very well known, you can include a short description in italics immediately under the organisation name (e.g., *One of the largest international software companies with sales of £...... and ..... thousand employees*).

10. **Achievements**

    These should be as relevant as possible to the role you are applying for, some qualitative (e.g. developed high performing teams) and some quantitative (e.g. increased sales from X to Y).

A prose profile

As an alternative or addition to a CV you might consider writing a prose profile. This might be up to two-thirds of a page long and describe you professionally (in the third person) in the first paragraph and then give a short history of your career in a few more paragraphs. The content might be along the lines of the way in which you might be introduced before you make a speech at a conference. The main advantage of this sort of format is that you have quite a lot of flexibility in the content depending on what you are using it for compared to a CV, which is more highly structured. It is also easier to make a prose profile be more forward looking – to reflect where you want to go.

Chapter 9

Networking

According to a LinkedIn global survey in 2017, almost eighty percent of professionals consider professional networking to be important to career success. Having worked with three hundred individual clients between jobs I am sure they are right – that has been my clients' experience too – so personal networking well is *essential* to you getting your next job – or portfolio of roles. It is also very important, in a very different context, if you decide to go down the entrepreneurial route and start your own business – the best prospects for your early clients are organisations and individuals you already know. (See Chap. 16).

What do we mean by networking if you are between jobs? Starting with what we *don't* mean:

- socially catching up with friends and colleagues

- going to a conference with hundreds of people and giving out lots of business cards
- working the room by shaking hands with most people at a party.

Networking in job search is *purposeful* – you are doing it very deliberately to help you find your next job – and you are doing it with people you already know.

So how do you go about it? First of all, you need to get all the contact details of the people you know in one place so that you can work with them. This might be in a single Excel spreadsheet or in a programme like Microsoft Outlook. Don't worry about how many contacts you have. You might be surprised once you start to list them systematically.

Then you have to organise them. Perhaps the obvious way is to think about who is most likely to help you find your new job, but there is a problem with this – you know who you know but *you don't know who they know* – and so it is actually quite difficult to organise your contacts in this way.

The second (and better) way to organise your contacts is to think about the *quality of relationship* you have with your network contacts. Which of them do you know really well, where there is a degree of mutual respect and who you have probably known for some time? These are the contacts that should be your priority for two reasons:

1. Because you know each other well, they are pretty likely to want to try and help you.

2. When you talk to them you won't need to be very polished in what you say about what you want and why you want it.

They know you well and so they are more likely to be more forgiving than a professional recruiter would be who is interviewing five–ten candidates a day and who will simply choose the person that he/she thinks is most likely to do the job well from a single, short interview. Talking with your contacts with whom you have a good relationship is therefore a *safe place to learn* and practise your communication skills.

Now you have identified the working equivalent of Friends and Family, what next? If you know them really well, you might just send them a text to arrange to meet for a coffee/drink, etc. and they will accept, probably without asking questions.

If you know them anything other than very well indeed, it is better to send them a well-considered email. The reason is that if you start explaining on the phone, they may be thinking: Oh, you are looking for a job. I can't think of any job that would be good for you. This is a bit awkward. In other words, they are thinking negatively, and their mind is closing down – when you want the exact opposite – you want to open up a discussion.

A well-considered email is therefore usually better for arranging the discussion than a short text or phonecall. The structure is something like:

- This is my position (I am leaving xxxx after working there for xxx mainly happy years).

- This is the type of job (or portfolio of activities) I am looking for – in not more than two sentences.
- Could we meet up for a chat because I would welcome your advice? (The word advice is quite important here because it is not threatening – indeed it is a bit flattering – and so your contact will be unlikely to feel they are being put under any pressure).

Your email must not read as if it has been cut and pasted and is part of a campaign. You should think about who you are writing to, what your relationship is with this person and tailor it to them.

And so, you meet up (which, of course, may be by Zoom call or equivalent) and after a bit of social catching up, the conversation is similar to your email (your current situation and the sort of role you are looking for). Then we come back to your *purpose* in networking. This is to see if your friends and colleagues can introduce you to people they know who might be relevant to your job search. It may be an organisation where they know there is a lot of change going on, or which is in a sector that you have experience in or just that they know people there who they are confident you would get on well with. They may, or more likely may not, know of a particular vacancy – if you can get to talk to their contact before a vacancy is advertised or given to a professional recruiter, so much the better – there will be less competition from other candidates at that stage, and you will have a head start.

This is how you go about networking: *doing your research through people you already know.*

Immediately you have had the conversation you should write short notes about it. After, say, thirty or so conversations along these lines you won't remember the details unless you are superhuman, and if you want to get back in touch with the same person sometime later, it will be embarrassing if you don't remember what you talked about.

Perhaps obvious, but still important, you should write a short email to say thank you for their finding the time to have this discussion. The people you want to see are very likely to be busy, and if you take up their time and then simply disappear, they are going to be irritated. (Many thanks for finding the time for us to have that chat. It was great to catch up. I will get in touch with xxxx as you suggested and I will let you know how I get on, so do let's keep in touch.)

This is by far the most likely way you will identify your next job. Of my clients, only about 17% find their next role through professional recruiters in the first instance and an even smaller number by direct online application, although what quite often happens is that they identify the opportunity through networking and then there is a formal recruitment process to go through.

How would you describe yourself as a networker? To some people networking comes pretty naturally, and they don't find it at all difficult. To many of us, however, it may feel a bit daunting and require quite a lot of effort. You will have to find a style of networking that works for you as an individual.

One thing to consider here is for you to think over the last five years or so, has anyone approached you and asked for your career advice? Maybe they felt they were at a career crossroads and did not know what to do for the best, maybe they were between jobs, or maybe they were currently in a role that they were really not enjoying. Perhaps you talked it through and helped them make a good decision, or perhaps you introduced them to an organisation or an individual who went on to help them. If something like this has happened to you, how did you feel when you realised that the discussion you had had been really helpful to that individual? Almost certainly you felt pleased that you had been helpful to them. Well, guess what, pretty much anyone who is able to help you in a similar way is also very likely to feel pleased about it, just like you did. And so, one way of looking at this is that by networking in this way you are giving your contacts a chance to feel good about their having been able to help you. Remember that research shows that helping people makes most people feel good.

In networking, you are almost certain to have good days and not so good days. You might look forward to meeting one of your contacts because you know they know lots of people. You come out of the discussion thinking, *well, that was a waste of time, wasn't it?* But the opposite is also true – you might approach a meeting thinking *this discussion is pretty likely to be useless.* It turns out that this individual was extremely helpful, generous with their time and contacts and introduced you to several people who were in turn very helpful. This might be because, although you did not know it, a few years ago they themselves had a difficult time between jobs, and they realised how important this discussion might be to you and so they put in quite a lot of effort to try and help. As one of my clients put it some years ago when halfway through his networking campaign: “It feels as if I am standing on a beach and the beach is full of pebbles. I know there is a gold nugget under one of these pebbles, but unfortunately, I don’t know which one!”

One question you should ask people in your network is whether they can recommend any professional recruiters they have dealt with in the past. This enables you to write to them saying that your contact suggested that you should be in touch. Professional recruiters are likely to be extremely busy people and if you write to them with the name of a previous client, or someone they know, they are much more likely to take the inquiry seriously than the emails they receive from the hundreds of people who write to their office every month with unsolicited CVs.

As part of your planning for your job search, you should set yourself a simple target for how many networking meetings you are going to try and achieve each month. The target should be realistic and make sense in terms of your own style of networking. The upper limit to this target is probably two networking meetings per day. You will have to prepare for each meeting properly, e.g. check out their LinkedIn profile (and, if their contacts are visible – do they know someone you would love to be introduced to?) You will probably want to check what you can find out about their organisation and previous organisations where they have worked. After your discussion you will need to follow up by doing some research on any individual or organisation they have suggested you should be in touch with. A target of, say, ten to twenty networking meetings per month might be a realistic target for many.

What happens if you feel you have exhausted the list of people that you know well or very well? This is reasonably likely to happen, but you should remember that your purpose is to get them to introduce you to more people and if, on average, each contact introduces you to one or two other people, your network will keep on expanding and then you will continue working with your contacts who you know less well. Your opportunity may well come from someone and somewhere you are least expecting.

The more people you have these discussions with the more likely you are to uncover an opportunity that will be good for you. By doing this you are creating your own salesforce, because the more people there are who know who you are and what you are looking for, the more likely opportunities will emerge from your network. Once you are well organised (e.g. in terms of your mission statement, CV and interview preparation and research on your target organisation), networking is likely to resemble a numbers game – the more networking discussions you have, the more likely you will be to unearth an opportunity. All my experience and that of my colleagues suggests that networking is likely to be a productive use of your time – even though some conversations appear, with hindsight, not to have been productive, one or two of them almost certainly will be.

You will need to work at networking. Done properly it greatly increases the chances that you will find a job that will be good for you and which you will be good at. You might also find that catching up with people you like but have not seen for a while is interesting and can be fun. On the other hand, you may well find that you have to kiss a lot of frogs to uncover a good opportunity.

Lastly, once you are in your new role, don't forget what you have learnt about networking, its importance and how to do it. It is better to develop and strengthen your network *before* you need it. If you are helpful to people in your network, more of them are likely to be helpful to you when you need it – and you never know when that is going to be. When you arrive in your new role, you have an opportunity to thank people in your network who have been helpful.

Chapter 10

The Power of Image

About the author

Melissa Lund is an image coach and personal stylist who has been working with companies and individuals since 1993 after training at London College of Fashion.

Melissa believes that image colours every interaction we have with the world. She says: "Image is a powerful tool and when we use it correctly it will enhance credibility, confidence and performance in any situation". Her clients come from many different sectors but share the need to look and feel as if they can take on the world and win. Sessions are energising and positive and the skills Melissa imparts to clients will last a lifetime.

The power of image

In the thirty years since I qualified as an image coach, I have seen many changes in my professional sector. When I started my consultancy, people thought that engaging the services of an image coach or personal stylist was something that only movie stars and other people in the public eye would do or could have access to. It was assumed that it would cost a fortune or that the advice wasn't going to be suitable for us "ordinary" people (and I'm using those quotes because frankly, no one is ordinary!) Companies were mainly interested in group sessions (obviously because it was more cost effective), when the real learning can only take place in one-to-one sessions due to the intimate nature of the work.

However, since I qualified from London College of Fashion in 1992, there have been a couple of shifts in perception about the image industry, one good and one not so good. The first – the good one – is that sometime in the early 2000s, people and organisations began to see that image is a valuable business tool and that there are many benefits to be drawn from doing work of this nature. The old notion that you shouldn't judge a book by its cover had seemingly been debunked. The second shift – not so good – is that some time afterwards – perhaps around 2012 or so, the pendulum began to swing the other way again with many people and organisations feeling that focusing on people's appearance was too invasive or could be viewed as politically incorrect. It's strange but true that during this time, I was hired for many jobs where the instruction was not to discuss someone's appearance, but the brief was obviously for an image review. This volte-face has, of course, coincided with a number of societal and cultural changes. I have no desire to make light of these changes because being more inclusive is only ever a good thing. However, I am not a believer in the "don't judge a book by its cover" theory and never have been. Evidence-based science shows us that this theory doesn't hold water for good reason. More about that later.

The truth is that image is a powerful business tool, but it is also a powerful force in life. In this chapter I'm going to set out what it can do for you and show you how you can tap into that power to derive incredible benefits which will last a lifetime.

Image – what's it all about, really?

Any work on image is always about getting the best response from everyone around you. In a business setting this equates to improving traction with the people who count for you, increasing visibility and therefore improving executive presence. If you do this, you'll be noticed in the right way. If you don't do this, you may be one of the many people who think that if they just work hard enough, and if they're good enough at the job, someone will notice them and give them that promotion, etc. We all know the world doesn't work that way.

Look good, feel good, perform well

The mantra in this work is always "Look good, feel good, perform well". I firmly believe that there isn't a person on the planet who doesn't want to look their best. Certainly, when we feel we are looking our best, we feel more confident, we perform better, and people respond differently to us. Confidence results in a growth mindset which aids mental well-being. A growth mindset encourages us to overcome problems and rise to challenges rather than lie down and get steamrollered by life and events. It is about taking control in a positive way, and as Mike has already mentioned, this is an important factor in developing and maintaining well-being. Research indicates that the people who are the most stressed at work are not senior executives with authority and plenty of autonomy, they are in fact people in roles with a ton of responsibility but without the authority to match.

Appearance and behaviours

Image isn't only about how you look of course, it's also about how you behave, in other words, it's about communication, both verbal and non-verbal. How do you want people to treat you? How do you want people to perceive you? How you communicate with people is important: what's your phone communication like, how do you manage video conference calls, what are your emails like? It all counts and all areas of your image need to be congruent. If you want to be perceived in a certain way, you need to look and behave in ways that encourage those thoughts. That doesn't mean that you should be doing anything that doesn't feel comfortable for you or isn't authentic for you. If you're uncomfortable in any way, shape or form it will show and people will feel less comfortable with you; you'll be perceived as less trustworthy. As Oscar Wilde said, "Be yourself. Everyone else is already taken."

A word about authenticity

Authenticity is an over-used word. Yes, I completely believe that you must be true to yourself, comfortable in your own skin, etc. However, that comes with a caveat: being authentic doesn't let you off the hook when it comes to manners. So many people think that being authentic entitles them to behave in whatever way suits them, without giving any consideration to anyone else. It doesn't. If I had a fiver for every time I'd heard, "Oh, they'll just have to take me as I am," I would have retired long ago! Yes, you need to show up as your authentic self but that doesn't mean that you can be late to the meeting, be unprepared (because you work best under pressure) and wear a Hawaiian shirt, shorts and flip-flops when a jacket, trousers and a great pair of shoes would have been the appropriate dress code for the meeting. Manners maketh man, so turn up on time (punctuality is the politeness of princes, so make that five minutes early), be prepared and be wearing appropriate clothes. It's about showing respect for the situation and the person you're meeting.

What is image not about?

I want to reassure you that image has nothing to do with vanity. I'm not disputing that everyone has some level of personal vanity of course, but the notion that if you decide to hone your image, or give it any attention at all, you're a vain and shallow person, doesn't chime with me. People who decide that doing the work in this area would be a good idea are people who have realised that it's a tool like any other and it's there to help us get where we want and achieve our goals. People who don't want to do the work are, frankly, missing a trick.

Strangely, fashion doesn't really come into play here, either. Fashion is a great thing if you love it (as I do). However, it's subject to the whims of culture and society in a way that image isn't. Image is about basic human response; it's about the lizard brain. If you're someone who really doesn't like fashion, clothes, or shopping then you're going to have to develop a strategy. If you ignore image, on your head be it because no one else will be ignoring your image, whether you realise it or not.

Having said that fashion doesn't play much of a part in this, it's important to look contemporary (which is not the same thing as being achingly trendy) particularly as we become more senior in business. In a nutshell, does someone wearing ancient specs (and I'm not talking cool, vintage Persol frames, you understand) look as if they know how the world works? I'd wager the answer would be no.

What can image do?

You can use image to improve the following areas:

- credibility, performance, and response
- traction and visibility

- diversity and inclusion
- confidence
- personal brand
- well-being

I'll come back to these areas later, but now it's time to discuss this science.

The science behind image

I like to anchor my sessions in science because it gives clients some context. The science behind image is Stone Age science. It's a gazillion years old but still holds true. The first tranche of research into image was conducted by the behavioural psychologist Professor Albert Mehrabian. Mehrabian, who is currently Emeritus Professor of Psychology at the University of California, conducted two studies in 1967, *Decoding of Inconsistent Communications* and"*Inference of Attitudes from Nonverbal Communication in Two Channels*, which were designed to ascertain the role of non-verbal communication in human interaction. He wasn't specifically researching image; he wanted to know how quickly one human being responded to another, and what helped people to make their judgements. Mehrabian's work has been misinterpreted by many practitioners in the image and presentational training business largely because people forget to stipulate that the 7-38-55 Mehrabian Communication Model (see below) only applies to the first few seconds, and it does not necessarily apply to the whole of a meeting or presentation. However, despite this constant misinterpretation, it would not be wrong to say that the results of Mehrabian's first two studies have widely become known as the science of a first impression.

Average response time:

- 40 seconds (or 30 seconds to a minute if you prefer a sliding scale)

Important areas:

- Appearance 55%
- Voice 38%
- Content 7%

If you're looking at these figures for the first time you may be shocked. You're probably thinking that you've spent the majority of time on content for the whole of your career and suddenly it seems as if the content is not that important. Actually, this isn't what Mehrabian meant at all. The figures above, which became known as the 7-38-55 Mehrabian Communication Model, indicate that non-verbal communication is more important than verbal communication *in the first few seconds* of contact with someone you've never met before. Mehrabian himself said that the percentages (although rigorously researched) were not set in stone but even if there's a certain level of flexibility here, at its heart Mehrabian's research demonstrated once and for all the importance of non-verbal communication in human interaction. People have tried to slice and dice Mehrabian's model over the years, but it isn't really possible because we have evolved about as far as possible as humans, so this model doesn't look like changing any time soon. The truth is that your content is massively important (whatever you're doing you need to know your brief) but unless you pay attention to the packaging, you are making it harder to be taken seriously. Mehrabian's research says that we have approximately forty seconds to be compelling. Since research tells us that people tend to go with their initial hunch about someone, it makes sense to do the work and do everything we can to make sure that we're on the front foot and giving ourselves a little competitive edge.

What's included in the areas?

Appearance: everything about you physically: gender, ethnicity, body language, facial expression, quality of movement, posture, weight, size and scale, hair (or lack of!), colour of hair, clothes, and accessories (including specs). It's also worth noting that handshake (which is your opening gambit) is part of this as well.

Voice: at this stage in the game (when you're walking into a room to meet someone) it's not what you're saying but it is about the sound of your voice. The vocal element scores highly in Mehrabian's communication model and with good reason – it's incredibly important. One of the first things we notice about someone is their perceived size and scale. Once we've figured this out, we have a good idea of the size of voice that will emanate from that person. If the size of your voice does not match the size of your frame, you're in trouble. The person listening will experience some cognitive dissonance and the result will be a delay in reaction time. Since we are hard-wired to respond quickly, anything that slows this response time is likely to make us feel uncomfortable; it's that lizard brain again! The automatic and speedy response we're hard-wired to produce gets held up. Since this is not what we're expecting, this can make us feel slightly less comfortable with the person we've just met.

Content: your wise words! Taking care of appearance and voice will allow your audience to take you seriously and ensure that they are ready to listen to you.

The Caveman Reflex

You can take the man out of the Stone Age, but you can't take the Stone Age out of the man. Mehrabian's model is what I call the Caveman Reflex as it is really about our fight or flight mechanism. It's perfectly logical because in that period of our development, we had to respond quickly to our surroundings and be able to evaluate potential threats to our social group. As bi-pedal predators, vision was our primary sense, and the visual field therefore gets top billing in Mehrabian's communication model. The vocal element is about sound and tone of the voice rather than words at this point. It gets second billing. Your wise words are last on the list because frankly, we're hard-wired to respond in about forty seconds and we don't have much time to listen to what someone's actually saying. So, this absolutely goes to prove that there's a point at which we do judge a book by its cover because we don't have anything else to inform us at that stage.

Every single one of us puts the Caveman Reflex into action whenever we meet someone new. When you leave your house or office every day and someone moves across your field of vision – and they across yours – two people are making a judgement about each other right there and then. It's most definitely a two-way street – it isn't just one person judging the other. It's worth noting that you can't turn this reflex off and you shouldn't even try to. The people who try to are the people who believe – erroneously, as it turns out – that what's on the inside matters in that first thirty or forty seconds. As I said, content is hugely important but if you don't tick the boxes in the right timeframe, you don't get a chance to connect on a more meaningful level.

The Caveman Reflex developed as a safety mechanism. These days, it still functions in that way, but it also allows you to figure out whether you want further engagement with someone you've just met. From the smallest thing – maybe meeting for coffee – to the largest thing – hiring them for your business – the Caveman Reflex is the starting point.

Acceptance and management are key

Given that our Caveman Reflex is something we can't turn off, management is a better tool than denial. Thinking about what image can do for you – how you can use it to your advantage, how you can manage it – is a good idea and a great starting point for improving image and personal branding. Time, then, to take a closer look at the areas I set out earlier in this chapter.

Credibility, performance and response

As I mentioned earlier, there's no substitute for knowing your brief. However, you can help things along by dressing and behaving in ways which reflect that brief. This is a shortcut to getting a great response because you are meeting people's expectations. The positive response you receive will in turn increase your confidence and self-esteem, leading to an enhanced performance.

Traction and visibility

When you're confident and performing well, getting a positive response from people, I guarantee you're going to get noticed by the right people in the right way. Visibility is increased. Hunkering down behind your laptop does you no favours. We all know people who think that if they just work hard enough for long enough, they'll get the promotion they deserve. Actually, I think most of us know the world doesn't work that way. Visibility is key to progression and showing up in the right way is essential to increasing visibility. What's interesting is that this tendency not to want to be visible can mean two different things. It can quite simply be a reluctance to put yourself forward, not realising that we all have to work to increase traction with the right people, or it can be related to a sense of entitlement and thinking that you're just so amazing at your job you don't have to bother with all that. Neither approach is helpful.

Diversity and inclusion

Whenever people talk to me about diversity and image coaching, I hate to say it but there's almost always a negative subtext, something along the lines of, "Well what about people who have a different cultural background? How does this work for them?" Well, it's no surprise that it works the same way as it does for anyone else. People are at risk of being marginalised for any number of reasons:

socio-economic background, gender, political ideology, ethnicity, education, etc. Working on image actually gives people who might be at risk of being marginalised the information, knowledge, and education they need to increase power and take back control.

Building a strong personal brand

The notion that we've all got our personal brand has been around for a while now, to the extent that the whole concept is at risk of being diluted. Personally, I think the notion of Brand You is still valid because at its heart, personal branding is about who you are and how you want to be perceived. Image (and specifically non-verbal communication) obviously plays a massive part in this as Mehrabian's research demonstrated.

Increase impact and presence

Some people are immensely charismatic. People want to be involved with them; people are willing to "follow them over the hill" so to speak. The rest of us may have to work a little harder. Working on all aspects of image can really help us to improve this area. Think about the qualities you want and need to express and how you're going to do this with your physical image. Clothes and grooming score highly here but so do body language, movement and posture. Height can be helpful, so if you're tall, make the most of it and don't dress to hide it or do anything to lessen your height. Height isn't everything though, so if you're not tall, use every inch you have and then think about quality of movement and body language. Moving slowly always helps. I don't mean at the pace of a glacial moraine, but stately progress. Take up as much space as possible when you sit down and use open body language. Don't attempt to make yourself look smaller. Posture is important so if you need to work on this, get started! Alexander Technique is the gold standard system for improving posture, but Pilates, yoga and dance will also help.

Using image to increase well-being

It's only relatively recently that mental health and well-being at work have become topics that are up for discussion. Employers have realised that happy employees increase productivity and give the organisation a PR boost as somewhere that's great to work, attracting the best candidates in future.

Mens sano in corpore sano is the Latin for a healthy mind in a healthy body, so the notion isn't at all new. I like to think this works the other way around too. Certainly, when it comes to coaching clients, my rather more prosaic experience is that a healthy body leads to a healthy and positive mindset. If a client really doesn't like the way they look, they will feel uncomfortable in their skin, and this will absolutely be a distraction from getting on with the job in hand.

Being at the centre of your own power

A while back, a client of mine described someone they knew as being at the centre of their own power. This sounded a little woo-woo to me, until I considered what it really meant and the implications it might have. Someone who is at the centre of their own power is comfortable in their own skin. They are not distracted by worrying about who they are, what they're wearing and how they might be perceived, because they have figured it out already. Being at the centre of your own power is akin to being at the eye of the storm. It's calm there – even if everything else is flying crazily around the edges – and being in that calm place gives you time to think about what happens next, how to react and what action to take.

How to be comfortable in your own skin

We know it's important to be comfortable in your own skin but how do we make it happen? First, let me say that none of us is perfect and perfection is not the goal. The goal is to be the best version of yourself that you can. I believe that everyone has an idea of how they'd like to look and if they can get 80% of the way towards that, then they're in a winning position! Personally, I'd like everyone to be able to pass the shop window test, that's to say if you catch sight of yourself in a shop window on the way to a meeting, it's important that you're happy with what you see. You need to be able to think, OK, that's good to go, now let's go and get the job done, rather than wondering why you didn't choose different clothes or why you didn't get a haircut! Honestly, you just don't need the distraction. In order to make this happen, you will need to take a good look at yourself and ask yourself what you need to focus on and what bothers you. Do this on your own. Don't ask anyone else. Above all, do not be hard on yourself; treat yourself with kindness and compassion as you would treat a friend. In my experience, distress can be caused by the following (in no particular order): weight, body shape and proportion, posture, ageing, teeth, nose, nails, ears and hair. Anything which makes you feel uncomfortable is not at all trivial. This is why it's not a good idea to ask other people about this. If it's a concern to you, it's a concern. If, when you look in the mirror, your eyes go first (and always) to the thing you don't like, then it's worth taking time to address that concern. The good news is that it's possible to improve pretty much everything. We live in an age where technology is our friend and there are so many advances in every field that, if we wish to, we can take advantage of them. Personally, I will never judge a client for being concerned about an aspect of their appearance. My aim is always to guide them to the best practitioner so that they get a result that makes them happy, increasing confidence, well-being, and performance.

If you have problems in your professional or personal life, working on image doesn't necessarily fix them all, I'll be honest about that. However, your clothes are your friends and your armour in life. If you're feeling anything other than your stellar best, being confident that you are looking your best can help and is not to be underestimated. You may have all kinds of issues that you're dealing with, and you may not want the world to know about them. Dressing to look your best will help you to continue to get the best response while you are working on the other things. The French have a saying which encapsulates this neatly: "If you change the outside, you can change the inside".

Menopause matters – for women and men

Menopause and its associated problems are now thankfully being openly discussed in the workplace. For many years, it was considered taboo to talk about this perfectly normal life stage – quite strange really when it happens to half the population who are of working age. For some women it's not a problem but for others it can be a difficult time. Hot flushes, night sweats, lack of sleep, mood swings, brain fog, lack of libido, aches and pains, weight gain, loss of muscle, depression. If it sounds bad, that's because for some women it is. Happily, HRT is now being more freely offered and many organisations are supporting women employees through menopause. According to an article in *The Times* in May 2022, 10% of women gave up work due to difficulties experienced during menopause. Companies are beginning to catch up with the idea – thanks to campaigners such as Davina McCall and Mariella Frostrup among others – that it's better to support women through this period in life rather than have them leave and take their valuable expertise and knowledge with them.

Menopause also affects men. Any behavioural and/or mood changes a woman undergoes will affect the men in her life, whether those men are romantic partners, business partners, friends, or family. When you don't feel like yourself, your behaviour often changes, and naturally the people around you are affected.

Andropause

Back in the Dark Ages, women went through the change (which was generally seen as a big and scary event and definitely not talked about in polite company) whilst men had a mid-life crisis, the cure for which was generally buying a sports car. Now, of course, we know that things are different. Men certainly have their own mid-life event – andropause. From the age of fifty, many men will experience a drop in testosterone with a resultant decrease in muscle mass, lower sex-drive, and potential for erectile disfunction. It's not all doom and gloom however, because just as women have HRT so do men in the form of testosterone replacement therapy.

The truth is that both men and women can suffer from unbalanced hormones from around 45 onwards. The answer to any problems you may be experiencing at this age, even if it's a vague feeling that something is not right, is to get your hormones checked to make sure everything is in balance. Sex hormones, cortisol and thyroid hormones would be a good place to start. You may need to have this done privately rather than rely on the NHS. A healthy diet and lifestyle, along with a positive mindset can also help to ensure that you feel your best during this transitionary period.

How to look your best

The biggest and most useful piece of advice I can give as a stylist is not to wear anything you don't love. It doesn't matter whether you're contemplating a T-shirt, a ballgown or anything in between; it doesn't matter if someone is telling you that your look fantastic, if you don't love it, it's not coming home with you. If you do buy it, I guarantee that this item will sit in your wardrobe rather than being something you will want to reach for time and time again. It will have been a waste of money!

That aside, when seeking to dress well, the first thing that needs to be considered is body architecture. Many people try to make this area complicated but there are in fact only three basic body shapes, with a couple of variations. The shapes apply to men and women, and they are as follows:

- **Inverted triangle**: shoulders and back wider than hips.
- **Rectangle**: shoulders and hips balanced.
- **Rectangle variation**: apple shaped with weight around bust and tummy.
- **Contoured**: shoulders narrower than hips.
- **Contoured Variation for Women**: pear shaped or hourglass.

It's important to remember that when you're assessing body shape you are not comparing yourself to anyone else. The only thing that's relevant is the relative measurements of your own body. For example, when someone states that they have wide shoulders, it's not about whether those shoulders are wide compared to someone else's, but rather it's about the width of the person's shoulders relative to the body underneath. The same applies to leg length. A tall person may actually have short legs if the legs appear short relative to the torso above, and a small person may actually have long legs if the torso above is short, relative to the legs.

Does body shape change with age?

The good news is that body shape is set by the proportions of the bones and those bones don't go anywhere, even if you gain or lose weight. So, no, basic body shape doesn't change over the years. If you started out as an angular person, you'll always be that shape. However, as we age, various things happen to the body and not all of it's good! We may gain weight, or if we stay the same weight, the weight may be differently distributed on the body, with more around the mid-section. In general, weight changes happen all over the body but depending on your morphology you may notice it in different areas. An angular person will probably notice gain or loss on the upper body, whilst a contoured person will notice changes in the lower half of the body.

We may find that our postural problems – round shoulders, tendency to slouch, forward head position, rounded upper back – have become ingrained to the point that they are making us look older and making it more difficult to get clothes to fit properly. We certainly will lose muscle tone. The answer to these problems of course is to work on what you can and don't panic about the rest. Pilates, Alexander Technique, yoga, and dance are all excellent for realigning posture. Working with weights and making sure your hormones are balanced properly (for men and women) will help you to maintain muscle mass.

Mid-body proportions

Mid-body proportions are crucially important when it comes to dressing well. Most people don't know about these proportions and that includes many of my fellow professionals. The two main distances in the torso are the nape to waist and the rise. The nape to waist runs from the nape of your neck to the anatomical waist; the rise runs from the anatomical waist to the end of your bottom. Interestingly, the waist is in the same position for men and women; the waist is the narrowest part of the body and it is the articulation point on the torso. If you ever want to know where exactly your waist is, bend sideways, put your finger on the point that's bending and straighten up, keeping your finger on the bend point. I will bet my bottom dollar that your waist is higher up the body than you think! For men reading this, note that your trouser waistband does not sit on your anatomical waist (not unless you're Simon Cowell, and frankly, that's a mistake).

These measurements are important because they affect comfort, aesthetics and fit. If you think about it, the waist is the narrowest part in any tailored garment (jacket, dress, fitted coat) and if the narrowest part of your body doesn't correspond with the narrowest part of the garment, it's going to feel uncomfortable and look slightly odd. The nape to waist length is not something that can be easily altered so if you've set your heart on something that doesn't fit in this area, you'll need to reconsider.

The rise is important because it can really throw out the balance of the body if it's too long. Too short is also a problem but this tends to look better aesthetically; if you've got a choice (which you don't, you're born with what you've got!), a shorter rise is better than a longer rise. A long rise, if not balanced properly with clothes, can make the legs look shorter.

Short waist/long waist versus short back/long back

Strangely, your back length (the nape to waist length) has nothing to do with whether you're short or long waisted. This term refers to the distance on the front of the body from the anatomical waist to the start of the bust. For this reason, it's one area which is more relevant to women than men. Many people think (erroneously) that they are short waisted if they have a short torso. They can be, but actually it's possible to have a short back and a long waist, or vice versa.

Having a short waist unfairly truncates the figure, and for women, can make us look rather matronly as we age.

Dressing a short waist

If you have a short waist, you'll need to create some space on the rib cage to balance your body. The following all help:

- **Underwear (women)**: get the best fitting, most supportive bra you can manage and replace it as soon as you need to. The aim is to lift the bust as much as possible to create a few extra millimetres (everything counts!)
- **Belts (women)**: never wear a belt on your natural waist as this will emphasise the problem. Wear your belts on your high hip. Drawing the line across the body here will make your waist look longer. Avoid wide belts in favour of narrower styles. A chain belt (Chanel-style) works really well too.
- **Waistbands**: avoid high rise waistbands and choose mid-rise, which will create extra distance between your waist and your bust.
- **Necklines**: if your short waistedness also means that your bust sits low on the chest wall (nothing to do with droopy boobs, by the way) then you'll need to wear lower rather than higher necklines.

Dressing a long rise

A mid-rise waistband will solve many problems as it slightly compresses the rise area by putting a horizontal line across the bottom, making it look shorter. Here's what you need to know:

Men

- Choose a mid-rise waistband rather than lower or higher.
- Make sure your jacket covers your bottom but is no longer than that.
- Make sure the distance between the top button on your jacket and the waistband on your trousers is not too great as this will emphasise the problem. If your waistband is midrise this will be fine.

Women

- Choose a mid-rise waistband for trousers or skirts. If you can find a style with a deep waistband, that will be great because this will shorten the appearance of the rise area.
- Avoid short and boxy jackets as this will make your rise look long from behind.
- Choose styles which skim over the area where your bottom ends and your thighs start. An example of this would be a dress in a fit-and-flare style, or a wrap or kimono style dress rather than a fitted sheath or a pencil skirt.

Legs

Long legs make everything look fabulous. In addition, they help us to look athletic and resilient, this is important when you have a major role because you need to give the impression that you can take on everything that will be coming your way, and then some. Not everyone is lucky enough to have long legs (in fact most people don't) but we can all make the most of every centimetre. Leg length is relative as mentioned previously in this chapter.

How to Make Legs Look Longer

- Waistband position on trousers and skirts is crucial; anything that makes the torso look shorter will make your legs look longer. Wear the highest waistband position you can.
- Trousers need to be the right length; too many breaks or too much fabric pooling around the ankles will stop the onlooker's eye from travelling up the body.
- Get the attention to the top of the body.
- Skirt and dress length can be either just on the top of the knee, or if you're going for a midi-length, make sure the hem does not cut across the widest part of the leg.
- Wear heels. Nude heels work really well to create endless legs, but they must be the same colour as your skin tone, so women with brown or black skin will need a different nude from someone with very pale skin. Nude shoes work with all colours of skirts and dresses but do not work with dark trousers.

Shoes

In general, keep your shoes the same colour or slightly darker than your hemline. For example, if you are a man wearing a charcoal grey suit (or jacket and trouser combination) your shoe choices could be black, dark brown or oxblood, depending on your personal choice and the level of formality you need on the occasion. They could not be tan or light tan as these two colours would cut the foot length away from the leg and you would then lose the opportunity to use the foot length to increase the leg length.

Think about the weight of your shoes, too. Wide trousers don't work with very lightweight, insubstantial shoes. Skinny trousers don't work with very heavy boots, or rather, they don't if you need to make your legs look longer.

Colour

In the early '80s colour analysis made its way from the US to the UK. Colour Me Beautiful was probably the first known proponent of colour analysis. Its initial offer was simple: people were divided into the four seasons of the year and given a palette, which corresponded to those seasons. This was known as seasonal analysis. Some years later, image coaching companies developed a style of analysis known as tonal analysis, which was based on the tonal colour theory developed by the Bauhaus group of artists. The results were more refined, standard palettes didn't exist, and any consultant with a set of drapes could mix an individual palette for clients. Tonal colour theory is logical, allows the client more freedom and generally gives people more colour education.

As a consultant who trained in tonal theory, I like this system for the flexibility it offers. After the widespread introduction of tonal theory, the seasonal theory consultants had to catch up. I don't think they did really; certainly, there was at one point a profusion of contradictory terms, indicating that they were paying lip service to something they didn't really understand: warm winter, for example. It's not technically possible to be a warm winter as a winter palette always has a cool undertone. Be that as it may, you shouldn't really get a different result, whichever system is used. There will, however, be different descriptors.

The important thing about colour is to remember the following: your profile is non-negotiable because it just outlines your qualities and indicates what will suit you and what won't; everything else colour-related is very much negotiable. The biggest piece of advice I could give you about colour, along with everything else sartorial, is don't wear anything you don't like.

Colour architecture

Colour is a great architectural tool and can be used to re-proportion the body when needed. If you want to look taller, shorter, slimmer or bigger, colour can help. If you want to create longer legs, colour is your friend. If you want to look youthful and healthy, wearing the right colours can help.

Creating gravitas and authority with colour

When you need to power up – a formal meeting, a big interview, a keynote speech, or presentation – you may decide that you need to look powerful. Tailoring is key but colour can also help you here. Go for the darkest colour in your palette and choose the highest contrast level you can. Authority figures through the ages have usually worn black and white and to this day, highly contrasting colours will allow you to create more gravitas than colours with a lower level of contrast. Use the lower contrast level if you need to look approachable. Colour is infinitely flexible.

Most people are drawn to the colours that suit them. However, they don't always know what happens when one colour is put next to another and when they put those colours next to their own skin. If this is you, a colour analysis session will point you in the right direction.

Colour and ageing

Your colour palette does not change with age but what may happen is that your skin, hair, and eye colour get a little lighter. If this happens, you may decide to lighten your darkest colours. For example, if you looked great in black in your twenties and thirties, you may decide that later in life you look better in dark navy or charcoal grey. Undertone and contrast levels don't really change. If you're a woman who decides to colour her hair lighter to offset maintenance time and costs, then be careful to stick with the same tone. If you are essentially a cool tone don't let the colourist suddenly give you a warm tone and vice versa.

Accessories

Never underestimate the power of accessories to add a little "Je ne sais quoi" to your outfit. Accessories elevate ordinary clothing to the next level, so they repay your investment a thousand times over. If someone's wearing a really great suit but their shoes are cheap and poorly maintained, the shoes are what will be remembered. On the other hand, someone can be wearing fairly basic clothing but if their shoes, bag, watch, and jewellery are outstanding, they will always be considered well dressed.

Accessories can make or break your look so think carefully about material, colour, and proportion when you're getting dressed.

It goes without saying that anything that goes with you to a business meeting and may be seen by others will say something about you as a person. Polished shoes and bag, an elegant belt if your trousers have belt carriers, a wallet that isn't full of cab and lunch receipts, it all counts!

Many people are seemingly accessory averse, but I think this is because they just don't know how to use accessories. To see the difference, choose an outfit you'd normal wear for a particular occasion and see how it looks with, for example, boots or casual shoes rather than formal shoes.

Finishing touches

The devil is in the detail when it comes to working on image, so don't forget to pay attention to hair, skin, make-up, hands, etc. Grooming is so important because it is always noticed.

Navigating dress codes

Dress codes vary across sectors and will, of course, depend on whether your organisation has a formal, business casual or a dress for your day policy. The information I've given here about fit, style and colour, etc. will work, whatever the dress code. What you have to figure out is what level of formality you need. I would definitely recommend dressing up rather than down if you don't know what the dress code is – it conveys more respect.

Post-pandemic, business dress has become increasingly casual. Actually, I don't think this was a conscious decision and I don't think it's the right direction to be going in. I think many people just started to think that since they weren't in the office, there wasn't a particular dress code that applied to them. In my opinion, I think that we always need to think about how we represent ourselves and our organisation to the best of our abilities, whether that's in real life or via a digital platform. Slightly more casual is fine but scruffy is not. It doesn't matter what you've got on your bottom half if you're doing a video call (as long as you don't have to get up to answer the door!) but anything we can see above the table does matter. A video call is still a business meeting – and you need to dress for this.

Conclusions

From this chapter, we can conclude the following:

1. Image is a powerful tool and managing it is a better strategy than denial.

2. It is pointless to stick with the "Don't judge a book by its cover" scenario because evidence-based science shows us that this does not hold water.
3. A strong personal brand is about authenticity: don't do anything (or wear anything) that makes you uncomfortable.
4. Building an image, which does you justice, can help you to increase traction and visibility.
5. You can use image to increase well-being.

In short, image is something that we shouldn't ignore as it is a powerful tool, which enables us to get the response we need from everyone around us. Who wouldn't want to tap into those benefits?

Chapter written by © Melissa Lund
(melissa@melissalund.com)

Chapter 11

Using LinkedIn and Other Social Media

About the author

Lincoln joined LinkedIn in 2004, back when the platform was still finding its feet with just over 100,000 members worldwide. By 2005, he was working with individuals helping them to understand the platform. To date, he has worked with hundreds of brands and organisations to help them make the most of the platform, as well as tens of thousands of individuals raging from students starting out to board members of FTSE 100 companies.

One of the reasons Lincoln can help people understand the platform is that he has spent over ten years helping LinkedIn themselves grow across Europe, Middle East and Africa and so he can explain the platform from all parties' perspective (LinkedIn themselves, what companies do on the platform as well as individuals) enabling him to provide a unique insight into the platform.

Why LinkedIn matters

At the start of the pandemic, Brunswick Group surveyed over 11,000 people on their communications expectations of corporate leaders across 13 different countries and markets.

From misinformation to employee engagement to crisis, the data is clear. Stakeholders expect executives to adapt to the changing circumstances they face.

The report spoke of the overwhelming expectation of leaders that they would use social media to be more accessible, transparent, engaging, authentic, and hence creating a new style of being a Connected Leader: engaging stakeholders directly through new forms of communication and on issues beyond the balance sheet.

Even though most professionals are aware of LinkedIn, it's not something many have taken the time to get to know properly, and as we know, being on something and using it well are two very different things.

What this chapter tells you about:

- How LinkedIn and the other social media tools will help you develop a network.
- How to create your profile.

- The importance of an online profile and the power of recommendations.
- How to search companies for someone who knows you.
- Using Groups and other social media tools to increase visibility and add value to your network.

LinkedIn is second to none when it comes to online networking. It helps identify the point of purchase (the person making the hiring decision), tells you all about them, and shows how you are connected to them. It also allows you, via email, to re-establish contact with those you haven't spoken to in years, without an awkward and possibly embarrassing conversation.

It is revolutionising the executive search industry, making head-hunters work harder to show the value they bring to a process as companies can also use it to identify and reference candidates. It has sped up the adoption of in-house recruitment teams, as organisations find they can significantly reduce their recruitment costs and build their own database of prospective candidates.

It is safe to assume that ahead of any networking meeting or interview your LinkedIn profile will be checked out on the site, either before or after. (It is also quite likely that your potential employer will check out other social media about you and so you should be careful not to post material that will suggest you might not be a good employee).

It is for this reason, if no other, that you should be a member of LinkedIn and give very careful thought as to how you present yourself on the web.

What is LinkedIn?

There are numerous websites out there aimed at helping you to network and share information. But over the years the one which has risen to the top of the pile for business purposes, is LinkedIn.

LinkedIn, as a site, was founded at the end of 2002 and launched in May 2003. For most people it is a site usually introduced to them by a colleague or close contact.

One of the original ideas for the site, was to allow users to create and develop their network, as they moved through their career. The site allows you to invite contacts to become a direct connection, and using a principle loosely based on six degrees of separation, it will allow you to view people in the first three degrees of your network who you know through common connections.

Starting out as an invitation only platform it has now grown to over 827 million members across 200 markets and territories.

Getting started: what to include and what to omit

There are a few things to remember when starting out – firstly your profile is never read by someone sat next to you; secondly, we have no idca why someone is reading our profile, and lastly it will be assumed that what you say (and how you say it) is based on how you want to come across.

For most people the starting point when using LinkedIn is to construct a profile based on your CV. But avoid the temptation to cut and paste information across from your CV. Under *no* circumstances do that. The reason for this is that your CV will hold information, which isn't designed for public view; secondly, your profile is keyword searchable, so only go into the detail around the areas in which you want to work in future. If you were once an IT manager but never want to work in the field again, only mention the role and the company with a small description, rather than going into lots of detail.

Your LinkedIn profile allows you to set out your stall. It is, in effect, the web version of your elevator pitch or mission statement. I would liken the information in your LinkedIn profile to being similar to what you'd tell someone over a coffee if meeting them for the first time.

Be familiar with all the sections available to you.

Starting at the top, create a headline (this isn't a job title but more about what you want to do), similar to a spine of a book. It will be what people see before fully viewing your profile and can create an expectation of what the reader will learn. Secondly, choose an industry that either relates to the one you want to work in, or to the type of role you perform.

For location choose the town, region, or country where you want to work (not where you live, if they are different).

Your next aim is to create a Summary or "About" section. This is likely to be similar to your elevator pitch. Talk about who you are and what you have done (if relevant) and what you want someone to know you are proud of. You can even discuss what you are looking for here. This section can include a heading and then a brief sentence to help set the context.

When it comes to experience, this is where you discuss current and past roles. Don't just add job titles and a company name. Some titles mean different things in different industries. You should go into detail about the jobs you've done that match your future aims, or the ones which help to prove relevant experience. Providing a sense of size, scale and scope can often be a good way to position you and what you have done. This is no time to be bashful – mention your relevant achievements. Focus on business benefits.

When writing the experience details, be mindful of length and consider paragraphs that are ideally no more than two sentences, or three-and-a-half lines in length. It's better to end up with four or five paragraphs that can be easily read and understood than one condensed paragraph, which blurs when read.

Under education, don't just list your school, college, or university qualifications, add some information on the subject, or titles of papers you have written.

For skills, we can add up to fifty, these can be endorsed or associated with particular roles. Please only list skills which are relevant and that you feel offer a breadth of your knowledge. Don't just play keyword bingo.

Volunteering can be a great way to introduce other areas of your life. These give the viewer an insight into your personality and are where you can talk about more than just bland facts or details. It can be a great way of showing another side of you, with the opportunity to link your business acumen to good causes.

Projects, awards, certificates and courses can also be great ways of adding small relevant details to your experience.

Photograph

It is essential you publish a photograph. If for no other reason than it will help those meeting you for the first time to identify you. It should be recent and taken in a style which reflects how you want to be seen. If your appearance is giving you cause for concern, visit an image consultant and/or get the photograph taken professionally.

Recommendations

We have always known that having met someone for the first time it is human nature to check them out. It's how we corroborate our first impressions. Of course, traditionally we turn to our network. LinkedIn very cleverly facilitates this checking out by telling you who you know in common. LinkedIn gives you the opportunity to get those who know you to give testimonials on your behalf. Having recommendations short-circuits the checking-out process. It enables those interested in you to see you and how they can connect to those in your network who are recommending you.

So how many recommendations should you publish? It goes without saying that no recommendations isn't a good thing. Avoid reciprocal recommendations, as it devalues them. Yes, it can be tricky to get a recommendation without getting one back, but get over it. You should look for two or three.

Ideally, it should be a former boss, a peer and a subordinate. Remember the most important people in your network are those with whom you hold a strong relationship and who are influential. You need these people to be advocates on your behalf. You should also consider getting recommendations from clients and suppliers. Former clients are of particular importance if you are in a business development role. Ideally, you are looking for sponsors who have gravitas within your industry and thus, by association, you too will be someone worth knowing. Your recommendations should always focus on specific results you have achieved. Like your CV, these should ideally be quantifiable. It isn't sufficient to say you are a nice person. Those checking you out need to see the tangible results you have achieved.

Groups

You only really want to connect to people you know. However, you can help shape your network by joining groups based on industries, locations and topics of interest. Check out the groups to which those already in your network are members. LinkedIn has thousands of groups. You are allowed to join fifty, so it is important you pick wisely. Think about your network and perceived weaknesses. LinkedIn groups give you the opportunity to develop contacts in those areas of weakness.

Groups will give you access to discussions, other members, career discussions and jobs. Whilst joining up to fifty groups might feel like a lot, you should at the very least join the groups relevant to your future career.

If you belong to a trade body, see if they have a group. If they do, then join it so you see what your peers are discussing. If you are looking to move industry then see what groups there are, which you might choose to join as a way to find out hot topics, issues and information about the industry.

Head-hunters will also create groups relevant to the industry or function in which they operate. Participation in groups is an excellent means of increasing your visibility. Remember that by sharing an update you are automatically updating your LinkedIn network.

Building your network on Linkedin

Once you've built a good profile the next step is to build your network. A network with fewer than 500 members is visible on your profile, once you go over 500+ connections then your network size won't be displayed. It's reasonable to think you would know a good number of people on LinkedIn. When you start to build out your network look for current/former colleagues, friends, family, and people you are happy to be associated with. In my opinion, you need a minimum of 500 people in your network. LinkedIn will suggest people you may know, based on what you tell it about previous employers and educational background. It does this each and every time you visit the site. So, allocating at least one hour per week to "play" on LinkedIn will quickly pay dividends as you build your network.

The site allows you to upload your contact from an email account, and then matches the email address you have on file with LinkedIn users and shows if they are already using the site. This is a quick way to grow your network. But a word of caution here: it is very easy to accidentally send an invitation to everyone. Make sure you don't.

The second option for growing your network relates to your profile. The site will match other users who have also stated that they worked for a company at the same time as you. This is a great way to find former colleagues. A similar method also applies to the education information entered by users.

Whenever you see someone you want to connect with, make sure you send a personal note with your invitation to connect; doing so is a great way to remind them of who you are, and helps you set out the context for your invitation. Given that you are sending an invitation, which you hope they will accept, the least you can do is say, "Hi, can we catch up?" or, "Great to find you on here, can we connect?" A personalised message additionally gives you the opportunity to add value to the recipient. This is the very art of networking.

There's another option available: "People you may know". This is made up of people who are connected to you by common connections, people you may have worked with and people whose email address you have imported.

You can review how your network is made up by viewing people on the site and then searching based on location, sector, etc. This gives you a good indication of how your network is spread both geographically and by industry.

The site helpfully tells you how many people have viewed your profile over a ninety-day period, you can then filter this "Interesting Viewers" Location, Industry and Company with action buttons like Follow, Connect and Message. This will allow you to reach out to people with messages such as, "Hey I saw you ...", spark conversations or build your network with your target audience in mind.

Job section

Companies pay to advertise jobs on LinkedIn, but it's not designed to compete with some of the more common job sites.

The search options are the same as most of the traditional job sites, with one difference. When you view a role, you are also able to see who you know in the organisation, based on your network. Also, if the hiring manager chooses to show themselves, then the site will show you if you know people in common.

You are then able to "get introduced" via the connections you have, and possibly use this to assist in your application.

The job section will also recommend roles the site feels might be of interest to you, based on what you state in your profile by industry, location and title.

Inbox

The inbox works in a similar way to a normal email inbox. Any message sent to you will appear here and some will also be sent to the email address you have registered on the site. You can also receive partner messages.

There may be three types of messages in your inbox. The first are messages received from your network, from introductions via your network or Inmail messages. These messages are also copied to your email account registered with LinkedIn. The second are partner messages sent by companies advertising products or services and promoting their business (you don't receive large numbers of these) and which are only sent to your inbox and not copied to your email account. The third type of messages are invitations to connect or link.

When you receive an invitation to link, it will appear in your inbox. You have four options regarding invitations:

1. The first is to accept (if you do this then the person is notified, and he or she will become a first-degree contact).
2. The second is to reply, without accepting (this allows you to send a clarifying message back to the sender, without having them join your network).
3. The third option is to ignore. By doing this the person doesn't know you have done this, and you can accept later.
4. The fourth option is to ignore and then report as I Don't Know. The person isn't notified you have done this and is used by LinkedIn as an early flag of inappropriate behaviour.

Companies

The "Search Company" option allows you to review information on a company, find out if you know anyone who works for that company (both directly and indirectly) as well as company descriptions, posted content, data on employees, and information on key employees.

You can also view useful statistics on employees. This shows details on types of roles performed in the company, length of employment, qualifications employees have and the levels of experience the staff have.

News

LinkedIn has editorial teams in key markets designed to provide you with trending news and insights based on you location and 'hot subjects'.

Using LinkedIn as part of your job search

LinkedIn's greatest ability is to help you be a proactive job seeker. By allowing you to target companies, you can search for more information about the point of purchase (the person with the power to hire you). It allows you to get vital background information about their work and education, their current role and perhaps most importantly, how you connect to them through your LinkedIn network. LinkedIn will tell you who you already know in that company. LinkedIn gives you the facility to connect to your network connection and ask for an introduction via email to the point of purchase. Without doubt the greatest users of LinkedIn are recruiters who pay for the facility to target job searchers. This facility is open to you.

You can follow companies of interest, and via settings, let the employer know you are interested in them.

Lastly, and perhaps most importantly, you can make it known in your profile that you are 'open to work' this will set a green banner on your photograph to show other members you are available. You can also set this so only companies who pay to use LinkedIn know you are open to a new role. Setting your profile to being 'open to work' will also create job alerts based on the titles you choose.

Other social media networks

Whilst for most of us, LinkedIn is a comfortable place to start networking online, make sure you consider if there are other sites you should use. These can give you the opportunity to establish your online presence, the ability to showcase your expertise and create the brand you wish.

Remember that people seeking you out will gather information from the internet, and with the tools available, learning about someone is a very simple process. Hence the need for careful management. Consistency and appropriateness of your personal brand are key.

Social media can also be a "light touch" vehicle to help build your network. Many of us are reluctant to establish contact with people we haven't seen for many years. We are fearful that they will suspect our motives, particularly if it is very obvious we are job searching.

However, I urge caution as this is a hand that can be overplayed. Too much self-publicity across the internet and you can lose your audience. Never use Twitter to stalk individuals. That said, social media is very much here to stay. It is a very important part of your job search and an essential part of ensuring everlasting employability. It is a great marketing tool for you that may well help you achieve your next professional role.

Also note that although I have focused on LinkedIn in this chapter, potential employers are also likely to check out your presence on other social media and so you should be careful about posting material elsewhere on social media that may raise questions about how good an employee you might be.

Chapter written by © Lincoln Coutts
(lincoln@lincolncoutts.co.uk)

Chapter 12

Preparing For Interviews

Preparation

Good interview performance will almost certainly result from thorough preparation rather than a happy accident. (Note: some of this material overlaps with Chapter 3: Who Do You Think You Are? but I wanted to have this as a self-standing chapter for readers who want to be able to dip in and out of the different chapters.)

The style of interviews in this chapter is that of the private sector. A style more typical of the public sector can be found on page 233.

Tips

Do enough research on the organisation to be able to ask intelligent questions. Gather as much useful information as you can from your contacts, Glassdoor, previous employees and any other relevant source.

Check the LinkedIn profiles of the people who will interview you.

Try to find out how long the interview will be and the likely format; try to speak to previous interviewees.

Dress as formally or informally as the photographs of senior people's LinkedIn profiles. Err on the side of formality as a sign of respect.

Good preparation enables you to focus on delivering your answer well, and build rapport with your interviewer, instead of visibly thinking and talking at the same time. (You are likely to break eye-contact if you are thinking hard and talking simultaniously.)

Be mentally prepared for unexpected questions (e.g. "What would you like your epitaph to be?" "Are there questions that I should have asked you but haven't?") Give yourself a few seconds to think, perhaps by saying: "That's a great question," before your answer.

You might be asked to make a short presentation on: "What would you do in this role in your first ninety days?"

Arrive fifteen minutes early and breathe deeply to help you to relax.

Body language: "Own the space". Sit up straight. Use your hands to emphasise, don't fidget or be over-relaxed. Lean forward to make a point.

You might paraphrase the question to ensure you have understood it correctly or follow your answer with, "Is that enough detail?"

Be prepared for an interviewer (e.g. a chairman or founder) that loves to talk about themselves and their organisation – you will then have to get your key points across very quickly and be prepared to interupt politely.

Don't be afraid of silence – answer the question well, succintly and shut up. Allow your interviewer to ask the next question. If you talk too much, or too rapidly, this will reduce your authority and impact.

Don't be afraid of paraphrasing the question to make sure you have understood it correctly.

Be the "best version" of yourself. Do not try to be someone you are not – most interviewers will smell a rat if you try.

Questions you should prepare for

1. **Tell me about yourself**

   Tips

   - This might be the first question you are asked. It is best answered in "bullet point" style – succinct, clear and structured. The rest of the interview can explore the issues in depth, but this needs to answer early on who you are and what you would bring to the organisation. Do not repeat what is obvious from your CV but summarise in a few sentences "What you would bring to the party" that would be very relevant to the role.

   - At this stage, you should focus on your professional, not your personal self. If the interviewer wants to ask some personal questions, they will probably come later in the interview.

- Think about what are the three things that you want the interviewer to remember about you and tell their colleagues that show you to be a uniquely strong candidate for this role?

2. **What are the achievements in the past five years that you are most proud of?**

   Tips

   - Prepare five varied achievements (not all quantifiable) to choose from.
   - The structure should be narrative: what was the situation, what did *you* do (i.e. *not* "we", "the company" or "the team") and what was the outcome? An interview is the one context where it is sensible and desirable to use the word "I". The interviewer is interested in what you personally did and what difference you made. Undue modesty in interviews might cost you the job.

3. **Why did you apply for this position? / Why are you a strong candidate for this role?**

   Tips

   - You need to have thought about the organisation's needs carefully – how can you explain why you are uniquely appropriate as a candidate?
   - Show enthusiasm – this is always good.

4. **Why did you leave your last job?**

   Tips

   - Keep this brief, impersonal and business-related. It must be non-defensive in tone (e.g. "I much enjoyed my time with xxxx. The new boss wanted their own team, so we discussed it and I left on very good terms"). You do not want to spend much of the interview on this issue or give the interviewer the feeling that you are difficult to work with.

5. **What are your strengths and weaknesses?**

   Tips

   - Identify, say, five possible strengths and choose three. Be prepared to follow up with evidence, ideally third party (e.g. This is what my last appraisal/boss/colleague said about me ...").
   - Strengths is likely to be followed up by a question on weaknesses. The one you offer needs to be authentic and clearly "non-fatal". Put the weakness in the past ("Early in my career I was told ... I took this on board and learnt from it and so now ..." etc.) Only volunteer one weakness.

6. **Give me an example of a difficult working relationship you have experienced.**

   Tips

   - What was the situation, what did you do and what was the outcome? What did you learn from this? Choose an example with a happy ending.

7. **How might your colleagues describe you? And on a bad day?**

   Tips

   - Be realistic, ideally supported by examples, e.g. from appraisals, comments from senior individuals. Tell a very short story (if you can) to bring the description to life and add credibility.

8. **What are your interests?**

   Tips

   - Unless you and your interviewer share a passionate interest, it is unlikely that you will spend a long time on this topic. It is an opportunity to show enthusiasm by talking about something you like and hence to build rapport.

Public sector selection process and interviews

The style of the selection process in public sector and quasi-public sector organisations tends to be different from the private sector and you would be wise to take this into account in your preparation. It is usually competency-based in approach ("Tell me about a time when ..." you have demonstrated this competence), is more likely to be highly structured and result in the number of points (literally) you are awarded during interview. It is likely that all the candidates will be asked the same questions.

This competency-based approach is widely used in central, local government, the NHS and charities. The rationale is that it is a fair and open process and capable of being audited, e.g. to demonstrate that an appropriate diversity of candidates has been fairly considered.

The style described below is typical of a public sector approach – but it will not be followed in every case and a more private sector style may be followed in some cases.

The process

The first part of the process (there are normally two stages) is usually run by head-hunters/recruitment agencies. As it tends to be more transparent than in the private sector candidates should try and work closely with the recruiters, e.g. ask them what they are *actually* looking for. The candidate's main role during the process is to "feed the evidence machine" – why you should be appointed in the light of the candidate criteria – usually outlined in the application information.

In general, the larger the pool of competing candidates, the more mechanical the process of selection in the early stages, e.g. experience criteria being strictly adhered to.

It is not helpful to try and fight what may be a quite demanding process – you have to try and work with it. The application form and the process will be very evidence led.

Look carefully at the person specification, which is usually competence based. You have to provide evidence in the form of mini case studies, ("I did ... and the outcome was ..."). It is important to provide concrete and not generic examples. It may be helpful to use some of the same words that are in the application pack. Your answers will need to provide some detail but be quite succinct.

The public sector sometimes welcomes informal visits. These can be useful as you can be shown around by a manager who understands the role, organisation and culture. Candidates may also be invited to have lunch with potential colleagues, whose comments will be taken into account in decision making.

The initial process and interview

A member of the panel may be made available for informal questioning by candidates before the formal interview. If this is the case, certainly contact them and arrange a conversation if possible – all intelligence is helpful. You may be offered the opportunity of a "fireside chat" before the formal interview. This may be decisive so you should take it seriously.

There will often be two or more people interviewing for the first stage of formal interviews; eight to ten candidates may be interviewed with a short list of three to five. References may be taken up before the interview, always by telephone. Referees may need to be available at short notice as the timetable is quite likely to be firmly adhered to.

The main role of the interviewers is to make notes on the evidence provided (which may be subject to audit) and so it is important that you come prepared and know the evidence you will provide. You should leave no room for ambiguity in your answers. The hiring organisation is likely to be risk-averse in its approach and so vague comments or generalisations are likely to be ignored or given low scores.

In the final ("Panel") interview there may be someone on the panel who is only there to check that the process is proper and who may not speak during the interview.

In general, the public sector is very open to applications from private sector candidates, although it is possible that, in particular organisational cultures, e.g. universities and the NHS, it might be that candidates who are clearly familiar with these specific cultures are appointed. Cultural sensitivity is key: demonstrating that you have been able to deliver in different cultures, e.g. through influence rather than authority.

Local authorities almost always use psychometrics, always for executive roles, less for non-executive roles. There is no right or wrong answer in psychometric tests. You have to work through them briskly and honestly (there are careful internal checks for consistency built into the tests and inconsistency will be viewed negatively). Some of the distinctions in multiple choice tests may seem very subtle.

Team engagement exercises

An increasingly common part of the selection is a form of "Team Engagement Exercise" or "Leadership Style Assessment", the purpose of which is to get an idea of how you might interact in practice with members of your potential team or employees from the wider organisation.

The members of this team may be members of your potential team or from the wider organisation. They may be asked to volunteer for the process. They may or may not know each other before the exercise and so you may need to affect introductions.

The format may be that you are asked to make a very short presentation to the team to introduce yourself.

Any member of the team may then be free to ask you any questions they like and a dialogue ensues.

How you perform in this exercise will be assessed by someone, probably on the final panel, who will judge the quality of your interaction with the team.

The final ("Panel") interview

The "Panel" process is often effective and usually quick, with conclusions sometimes reached on the day of the interview. There may be two to seven people on the panel. The overall style is likely to be more formal and structured than the private sector with the panel sometimes sitting behind a large desk. It is wise to err somewhat on the side of formality.

Although you are likely to be asked about how you meet the criteria in a structured way, it is still important that you give the impression that you are the sort of person that they would like to work with, that you would fit in.

The successful candidate is likely to be the one that gave the most and best examples, best expressed in the time available. Thorough preparation, including knowing the relevant numbers associated with your examples, is required. Part of your preparation will include checking the background of each of the panel members. You may be able to call a relevant HR person in advance. In any case, you will be expected to demonstrate thorough preparation, e.g. by demonstrating knowledge of the local community.

The process can be formulaic, with all the questions predetermined as interviewers go through the criteria with each candidate. It is likely to be more of a question-and-answer session compared to what might be more of a dialogue in the private sector. Typical duration would be forty-five minutes with fifteen minutes between interviews for note-taking. Timing is quite likely to be adhered to. The head-hunter may even be prepared to provide guidance on the panel and questions likely to be asked in advance. (There are even recent cases where all candidates have been provided with all the questions in advance.)

Before the interview starts:

- check the background of each of the panel members
- be nice to the receptionist – panel members may ask them for their impressions of you
- read the brochures, newsletters in reception.

The interview:

- Don't bring anything else into the room (coat, bag, etc.) as it may be awkward.
- You may shake the panel members' hands.
- The panel chair will probably introduce each panel member.
- Be guided by them for the pace.

- They are likely to have different levels of experience of interviews – but all panel members are likely to have been formally trained in interviewing.
- They may begin with softer questions.
- Each of the key criteria/candidate requirements is likely to have been divided up amongst the panel members for them to ask you.
- You must demonstrate respect for all of them – your job is to get as many "votes" as possible – treat each person as an individual and be careful to balance eye contact with each member.
- It is OK to ask for clarification and ask if the answer was OK ("Was that enough detail?")
- Panels may use "hard cop/soft cop" routines.
- Don't be afraid of pausing to think – and then give a better answer.
- It is OK to take some notes.
- You should ask questions that demonstrate you have prepared well and looked at any relevant documents in the public domain, (e.g. key policy statements, press releases, annual reports).
- The things you do at the end of the interview, (e.g. your questions, the way the discussion is brought to a close) are likely to be influential.
- Do not ask questions about process – you will be expected to know that.

- Do not ask about package – if you are offered the role there may be some room to negotiate but it is likely to be fine tuning.
- They will all have the same form to fill out to score your performance.
- You may conclude by offering to leave a copy of the presentation if you have been asked to make one, (e.g. a ten-minute presentation on "How I would address the challenges faced by this organisation").

What if You are Not Successful in Your Interview?

Many of my clients become quite concerned if they don't hear quickly of the results of their interview. It is always sensible to follow up with a positive email shortly after the interview, saying how much you enjoyed the discussion and how you are looking forward to hearing from them.

If you don't hear, say, within ten days, this is not necessarily bad news. You probably have one thing on your agenda (getting your next job) but your interviewing organisation very likely will have lots of different issues on their agenda, most of which you will not know about, e.g. maybe they are considering a major acquisition, one of the key decision makers is off sick, they are reconsidering what they really need in the light of the candidate interviews.

By all means follow up politely and positively after an appropriate interval but don't nag.

If you are unsuccessful in your interview, it could be because you would genuinely not have been a good match for this organisation. Being unsuccessful in one interview has little bearing on whether you will be successful or not in the next, so don't be easily discouraged. It is quite likely that you will not be given much feedback about why you were not successful. See if you can get any feedback and move on positively to the next opportunity.

You probably should not wait for the outcome. Immediately after the interview get on with preparing for the next prospect.

Chapter 13

Your Campaign Plan

Once you are well prepared, e.g. you have your mission statement prepared, your CV and LinkedIn profile are in good shape, you are ready to be interviewed, you have organised and are pursuing your approach to personal networking, then you can seriously begin your campaign to search for a new role or roles. It is helpful to think of organising your job search activities as a campaign or a project, and to follow the discipline of writing down a plan, probably on a single sheet of paper. This is partly because in your previous role within an organisation much of your day would have been structured and meetings and activities would probably tend to appear in your diary and hence provide a considerable amount of structure to your day automatically.

Now you are in a position when you are looking for your next role(s) you will have to provide much of this structure yourself to help you work in a more motivated, effective and focused way.

Your mission statement

At the top of your campaign plan is your mission statement. (Chapter 7.) This is at most a two-sentence description of the type of ideal role you are looking for. It is crucial that you have considered this carefully in the light of your main skills and motivations so that the person you are speaking to is very clear about what you are looking for – so that you make it very easy for them to help you. If you are not clear by being too vague, or by giving more than two options of types of roles you might look for, you will make it very difficult for people to help you. It is possible that you may have more than two options and that you might use a different choice of two options depending on who you are talking to.

Your mission statement drives all your conversations with your network contacts and recruiters and is the answer to the question, “Ideally, what are you looking for?” It will also, perhaps in a slightly different form, be included in covering letters and possibly in your CV.

Organising your diary

It is important that you organise your diary so that you know when you are working on your job search and when you are not. It is not going to be helpful if you are sitting at your computer waiting for responses to emails if you are thinking you could be out with your friends or family. Equally, it is not helpful if you are out with your friends thinking that you should be checking your emails. Being clear about this by structuring your diary will be psychologically helpful and help you stay focused and positive. If you are largely working from home, it will be a good idea to organise a particular physical place where you do this work, if it is possible for you to do so.

It could be that you will do this work in the mornings, or maybe Monday through Thursday – whatever pattern of work that works well with you.

Key Performance Indicators

Your job search has many of the characteristics of a project: it has a clear purpose, may be of limited duration (maybe six to nine months at senior levels where there are not many jobs), it has time and resources dedicated to it (mainly you), and it needs managing effectively. You should also therefore consider what some of your Key Performance Indicators (KPIs) might usefully be in your job search.

They should be quite simple, and you may want to choose your own. I would suggest you consider two:

- How many personal networking meetings are you going to have as your objective per month? This will vary with your style of personal networking, but it should be achievable by you. Perhaps ten a month or more.

- The date by which you will have been in contact with all the recruitment organisations you have as targets. If you can manage it, it is always best to have a personal introduction to recruitment agencies as they will take more notice of an introduction, say, by one of their clients than they would of an unsolicited CV. ("*Anything is better than a cold call.*") You should not try and write to them all at once as you will want to be able to learn as you go along and the more well-considered and tailored your email looks the more likely they are to take some notice.

Your campaign plan should not be inflexible or elaborate but it will provide your job search with a useful framework and should help you manage your time effectively.

Chapter 14

Onboarding – Your Ninety-Day Plan

You may be asked to present a short "Ninety-Day Plan" during the selection process, or you may develop it early in your new role. This could be a plan that you develop mainly for yourself, or that you choose to share with your boss. If it is required during the selection process, the underlying purpose is to show what you, and you uniquely, will bring to the organisation that should create value whilst also revealing something of your style of working. It should put in the mind of your selectors a good picture of what working with you would be like. It will comprise of issues that you might consider and work on during your first three months in the new position. Your own style and priorities will be different, as will the organisational context, but what follows is a checklist to think about. Your plan needs to be something that you, and others, will get excited about because you will experience unanticipated challenges in trying to achieve it. The underlying purpose of your ninety-day plan is to persuade the selectors that you are uniquely well qualified to be appointed, although it should not say this directly. Of course, anything you put in your ninety-day plan will need to be something you think you will have a realistic possibility of delivering in practice.

It might be helpful to think about your ninety-day plan at least as much as a process, (e.g. of consultation) as your producing a document. For example, you might determine, re stakeholder management, that you would identify all of the key stakeholders before you start in your new role, that you would aim to have met them all and identified their priorities by day thirty, then integrated their objectives into your plan to the degree possible by day sixty. Outlining a sensible process is less risky than coming to definitive recommendations – when you are still outside the organisation and when your audience may have quite different views.

(Note: my underlying assumption with this structure is that you will be in a senior role in a private sector organisation but many of the questions will also apply to the public sector.)

Here are some of the headings you might consider in the preparation of your ninety-day plan.

Understanding the market

- The Unique Selling Point (USP) of your business versus that of your competitors – is there one, what is it? Do you understand how best to exploit it?
- What are the key trends in the market? Have you been gaining or losing market share? Do you understand why?

- Do you know who your key competitors are and their strategies?
- In the light of market trends, what needs to change for the company to thrive?
- What might kill the business? How can this risk be mitigated?

Key business issues

- How can they be identified? Can you identify ones that others have not?
- What is the received wisdom on these issues? Is there evidence for this? What more evidence do you need on what the real issues are?
- Which issues are both critically important and urgent?
- How will you get agreement on what the key issues are?
- How is your organisation managing climate change issues?
- What is non-negotiable for you, and for others?
- How will you prioritise?

Strategy

- What is the real *purpose* of this organisation? Is it understood and agreed upon?

- How is your business going to win if your plan is followed and why should anyone believe you?
- What is *really* in the interests of the business in your view? (This may not be the received wisdom and may not be popular.)
- What is the supporting rationale, and can you provide critical facts?
- Are you paying sufficient attention to getting buy-in from key people before asking for formal approval?
- How much capital will you need to get this done? What will be the effect on sustainable profitability?
- How do you make this fit with public statements/ group strategy?
- If you are confident about your strategy and you have buy-in, what are the first three things you have to do?
- What if this doesn't work? How will you know?
- What is your overall plan for the next twelve months?

Finance

- Do you really understand how you are making/ losing money in this business?
- What are the critical financial Key Performance Indicators (KPIs)? Are there important things that are not being measured?

- What can you do that will improve performance?
- What are the board's expectations? Are they realistic?
- Are cashflows roughly equating to the accounting presentation, e.g. does free cashflow roughly equate to growth in profits? Are you sure you understand how cash comes and goes? Does the present use of cash make sense?
- Are you confident there are no black holes in the finances? What do the auditors say privately?
- What is the state of the balance sheet? Does the organisation have enough reserves to do what you believe needs to be done and get you through some unforeseen delays or difficulties?
- Does your authority level allow you to get done what you believe is necessary? How would you seek further authorisation?
- What are the key financial risks? Are they being mitigated?
- What are your outline aims in terms of growth in turnover, margin, profits and return on capital?
- What costs can sensibly be reduced?
- How will shareholders be likely to react to your plan?

Risks

- Do you have at least an outline understanding of what the key risks are in the business?
- Are there ways you could suggest to best manage or minimise them?

Stakeholders

- Aims, perspectives, politics, power relationships – do you understand them? Do you know who really calls the shots?
- How will you consciously manage the key stakeholders?
- How do you make friends in this organisation and minimise the enemies you make?
- How can everybody win? (Assuming that everybody can win – it's not guaranteed.)
- Are you clear about the difference between being liked and respected?
- Do you have someone that you trust who can explain how the politics really work here?

Regulation

- Do the regulatory professionals understand the key issues and have a grip on them?
- What are the key regulatory risks and are they being managed?

- Are relationships with key regulators reasonable? How might they be improved?
- What are the implications for the regulatory framework in terms of how you do business?

Team development

- Triage – are there people who really need to go? (Typically, where you consistently have to supply more energy than they generate.)
- Gap analysis – who are you going to recruit/fire so you turn what you have into what you need to deliver the strategy?
- Do you understand the key motivators for each of your team?
- Is there political or other behaviour that is not acceptable to you? How will you deal with that?
- If you need to remove people, how will it be done? Is that the way you would like to be treated if it was you?

Key relationships

- What are your aims?
- Who do you like/dislike, trust/distrust? What can you do about that?
- How can you increase the number of your allies without compromising you, your values or the interests of the company?

Plan development

- What about your plan is private to you?
- What is to be shared with your boss/team?
- How do you build ownership of your colleagues to your approach?
- Numbers (financial and non-financial)/process/operational KPIs?
- Do key processes need to change?
- What is the timetable for your chosen KPIs?
- What are the critical milestones at thirty, sixty, ninety days?

Culture

- Do you understand the key unwritten rules about how business is done around here?
- What degree of challenge is acceptable? Do sacred cows need to be slain? How will you go about this? Who do you have to get onboard?
- What culture do you want people to associate with you?
- Are you happy with the ethics and behaviour of the organisation? What needs to change? How do you get buy-in to this?

Personal

- What are you *really* motivated by?
- What do you hate? How can you minimise your exposure to that? Can someone else take care of this?
- What or who might derail you? How can you reduce the risk of failure in your role?
- Are there ways that you can make your work-life balance manageable?
- Health: what do you need to do to look after it?
- Family: how does your family feel about your working life? Is that OK for you?
- Is this role taking you in a direction you want to go in? What needs to change if not?
- Is this the right place for you? How much time will you give yourself to come to a view on this?

Reputation

- What do people know about you now?
- What should they know?
- What do you want people to be saying about you in three months when you are not in the room?
- Because people will often pay more attention to what you do rather than what you say, what is the first action that you would like people to pay attention to?

Chapter 15

Retiring? Designing The Next Part of Your Life

Unpacking your skills

The priest in our local church announced one Sunday that the church would have to close because it was financially insolvent. A number of the parishioners had considered the issues carefully and this was the conclusion that they had come to.

I thought that that would be a shame because the church had been making a positive contribution to the local community for a long time. Since I had been working as a company doctor for the last five years or so – going into businesses that were in financial trouble and seeing if I could help give them a positive future – I offered to have a look at the figures and see if I could propose any ideas.

A few days later I sat down with a group of parishioners and began to look through the figures. Everyone was helpful and very concerned but none of the other members of the group had a business background. After a couple of hours, I said:

"Obviously the church is very short of money, but as far as I can see, it is not insolvent. A few years ago, the church took out a loan to pay for a new central heating system. There are only two months more payments to make and then the ongoing costs will be significantly reduced. If we can persuade as little as four of the parishioners to make their weekly contributions after their declaring Gift Aid, we will get a rebate from the taxman and the church should be able to continue." I was asked if I would be happy to make a presentation with other members of the group to explain this to church officials so that the matter could be reconsidered. We did so and the church was able to continue to provide a service for the local community.

This is a simple example of how some of the skills that you have acquired in your working life, and that you don't think about, can be very helpful in a completely different context. It is a matter of giving some reflection to the sort of skills and experience that you have – unpacking them – and then thinking in what sort of situation might they be helpful. This is one way of beginning to think of things you could usefully do in "retirement".

"Retirement"?

In the working lives of your parents, and their parents, life probably consisted of three quite clear phases: their education, their working life and their (probably short) "retirement". With the significant increases in life expectancy, and a much greater degree of fluidity in working lives, the "retirement" phase has got a great deal longer. With good fortune and carefully looking after our own health it would not be unusual for individuals to have about twenty years of relatively good health after they "retire". In short, I don't think that the whole idea of "retirement" is a very helpful concept or describes well what many of us will do after the end of our main working life. (Read Lynda Gratton and Andrew Scott's thought-provoking book, *The 100-Year Life: Living and Working in an Age of Longevity.*)

Of course, if you are able to design and then create the next part of your life, you will be particularly fortunate. Many will not be able to do so for pressing financial or health reasons. But given a long enough time to make progress towards your chosen destination, it may be that you have more freedom than you first thought.

Ex-policemen helping Afghan refugees during emergency evacuation

For example, I am a non-executive director of a business called GSA (see Bob Quick's experience in Chapter 16), which mainly consists of a flexible workforce of "retired" policemen. The retirement age of many policemen was, until recently, forty-eight. There is therefore a large body of highly trained individuals who are used to dealing with very difficult situations, acting on their initiative and dealing with a wide range of people. GSA was able to mobilise some 300 ex-policemen to help some 12,000 Afghan refugees during the recent emergency evacuation from Afghanistan. The refugee passengers were arriving day by day, usually with only the clothes on their backs, traumatised by their recent experiences and needing food, clothing and support. Babies had been born on the flights, there were untreated bullet wounds and there were unaccompanied children as well as significant physical and psychological welfare needs. The GSA welfare teams – the ex-policemen – very quickly organised local charity collections of clothes and shoes and collected Trauma Teddies, for the children, for which the refugees expressed their very sincere gratitude.

This is a very good example of how using the skills and experience of "retired" individuals in a different context can be highly constructive. It just requires some imagination to see and exploit the opportunity.

A long and healthy "retirement"

I keep using quotation marks around "retirement" because, for many of us, it may be a new, exciting, and constructive phase of our lives. It is quite possible that the mortgage will have been paid off, and if we have children, they will hopefully no longer be dependent on us and some of us will be under less financial pressure than for many years for these reasons.

An old friend of my mother used to say: "Eat your nuts while you've got your teeth." Good advice! Or as one of my clients put it in more professional language, it is all about, "the quality of life remaining".

For many of my clients who are in this admittedly fortunate position the challenging question is therefore: "What are some interesting things that I can – and want to do – now and how can I spend time with interesting people doing things I like?" As the above examples show, the range of things you can do may be much wider than you have had to do during the main part of your working life.

One or more than one thing to do? Designing the "components of your Portfolio"

During the earlier parts of your working life, it is quite likely that you were mainly engaged on one full-time job and that your employer would not allow you to have more than one role.

In this phase of your life, it is more likely that you will be able to pursue more than one activity. You may wish to develop several components of this new portfolio phase of your life, for example:

- **Family and friends:** Do I have an opportunity to spend more time with my family and friends than I have had previously? Will doing what I am thinking of doing give me the opportunity to invest in relationships with people I want to spend time with?
- **Giving back:** Do I have time for, and am I interested in, some form of giving back? Could you give some of your time, energy and skills to an organisation whose purpose you identify with? You can give some thought to what skills you can use that would be of most use to the organisation you want to work with. You could work in a soup kitchen for the homeless, which I am sure would be appreciated, but if you could use your business skills to help your charity make a successful application for lottery funding, that would have a much more beneficial effect on your chosen organisation and their clients.

- **Volunteering:** It could be that you gain a simple pleasure from helping out at the local riding school with classes for disabled children and that is fine – you are enjoying living in the present, with no other goal in mind. Giving makes most people happier than taking.
- **Paid work:** Are there opportunities for you to work, maybe on a paid consultancy basis, to use the skills and experience you have built up over the years?
- **Hobbies:** It might be that you used to have a hobby in your younger days that you could now pick up again – or find a new one. You might like the opportunity of being able to travel more.

How do you go about achieving your "ideal" portfolio?

Many of the approaches that I have discussed earlier in the book are very well-suited for designing this part of your life. You can apply them here, not least because you are likely to have more freedom to design how you want to spend your time than earlier in your life when family and financial imperatives were probably a lot sharper.

In designing the components of your ideal "retirement" portfolio, you can therefore consider:

1. What can I learn from my past about what I will probably enjoy in the future?
2. What actually makes me happy?
   - Having a sense of purpose?
   - Investing in relationships?

- Being in control of my life?
- Living in the present?
- Exercise that I enjoy?

Research shows that if you pay attention to these factors and score relatively highly on them, you are more likely to have a longer and healthier life and be more productive.

3. Creating your preferred working future. You may well have more scope to do this now than you had earlier in your career and may be able to take a longer-term view now the immediate financial and family imperatives are dealt with.
4. When I am talking to friends and colleagues, what is my "mission statement" that will make it easy for them to help me?
5. Is now the time for me to start that business I have always been thinking of but never been able to pursue? (Lots of successful businesses are started by entrepreneurs who have a lifetime of business experience but have never before been their own boss.)
6. How do I use what I have learnt about networking to achieve my portfolio?

Negotiating with your partner

If it has been the case that one of you has been working in a very time-demanding role while the other has had a less time-demanding role, it could be that as your "retirement" from your very busy executive life approaches, you will need to discuss with your partner in broad terms how you will spend your time both separately and together. This may well be a big change in at least one of your lives. (*"I married you for life, but not for lunch!")* It may be that this is happening in addition to the readjustments involved in experiencing the empty nest syndrome as any children have grown up and place much lower demands upon your/your partner's time.

It could be sensible to jointly do the exercise in Chapter 5, "Consciously Developing Your Life Vision" as a more structured approach to jointly addressing these issues.

Time management/IT skills

If you have been used to your diary being structured at least a month in advance and that someone else has effectively been managing your diary, you might find it a bit of a shock to be looking at a diary, which is almost empty.

It could be quite an exciting process choosing to mostly fill your diary with experiences, which are mainly of your choice. It may also be that you have to become more skilled in terms of using one or more electronic diaries, setting up virtual and face-to-face conversations and hence managing your time so that you enjoy the balance of what may be very different activities. No one else will now do this for you. (Personally, I have resorted to an old-fashioned paper diary as I think this means I am less likely to miss something from my several electronic diaries associated with several different email addresses.)

Getting there

It could well be that it takes you several years to work out what you really want to do in this phase of your life (more slow thinking) and start putting these different components together. That's fine – think of it as an adventure you have never previously had the opportunity to enjoy. You can enjoy the journey, and not just the destination.

A brainstorming exercise

In thinking about what you want to do over the next few years, it may well be a good idea to challenge yourself with a brainstorming exercise.

You can list thirty to fifty things that you can explore. Don't evaluate them, just create a list, maybe with the help of someone who knows you well but ideally who has a quite different background than you.

You don't have to do this at one go, start the list and keep adding to it, don't stop until you get to at least thirty, and preferably more.

Then you could apply the well-being lens – which of these (or which combination) is likely to make you happier?

Then you could apply the energy test – which of these ideas really energises you? You can look down the list and simply choose the top three that really excite you ("Wow, wouldn't it be amazing if I did that!")

Then, importantly, start today – take the very first and small step towards your goal. It can be tiny but do it *today*. If it makes you feel good, take another step tomorrow.

Of course, the list will also have to have some basis in terms of practicality. On the other hand, given enough time and determined application, you may well be surprised what you can do. (At the age of sixty-eight I gave my first TEDx talk; at the age of seventy-one I am writing my first book and I have recently won my first photography prize.)

Have I been following my own advice? My own portfolio

You might be thinking, and it would be a fair question, am I following my own advice? (You can, of course, skip this part of the book if you mainly want to focus on developing the skills and approaches I have outlined above).

The answer broadly is yes. Life is rarely tidy: friends get ill or sadly die, finances have to be managed and things arise in the world like the Covid pandemic that turn our lives upside down, at least for a while. Below are the components of my current personal portfolio. Yours, of course, will be very different but you might notice how some of the things I do appear to follow the principles of happiness I described in my TEDx talk a few years ago.

1. **Friends and family:** I now have four grown up "children" who are all pursuing quite different lives and who are a source of great pride and pleasure to me. (It was mainly my wife who made them what they are while I was busy pursuing my executive career.)

2. **Using my skills and experience working with people I like:** I have several parts of my portfolio

that have taken a good few years to create but which I enjoy:

- **GSA:** working with one of my clients from more than ten years ago to help a security business grow. (This was the business that helped more than 12,000 Afghan refugees.) I am very pleased to be associated with this project and this business. GSA is also very successful in financial terms.
- International Centre for Executive Options (ICEO): I still work with senior executives and help them work out what sort of role, or roles, they are likely to most enjoy and most likely to be effective at. It gives me much satisfaction when I am told, as I am reasonably frequently, that they have achieved their "dream job" and that I have made a positive difference to their lives.
- Autolomous: I have been business adviser to the founder of Autolomous Ltd. that developed a software platform using blockchain technology that enables client organisations to take blood samples from patients with rare diseases, genetically modify the T cells and then put the blood back, often into the same patients. Then the T cells attack and hopefully cure the cancer. Clients' organisations literally save patients' lives, which can be a powerful motivator.
- OfficePOD: I am chairman of OfficePOD Ltd. that makes ergonomically designed modular

offices that can be installed in twenty-four hours, making good use of ways of more flexible working, and reducing the carbon footprint of working.

- Future Work Ventures: I am adviser to a group of companies, including start-up and turnaround prospects, that have the future of work as their overall theme. ("Shaping the Future of Work" may be the theme of my second book.)

3. **My hobby – photography:** I have recently taken up again my interest in photography, which I used to do in my late teens (mikeasmithphotos on Instagram). This is a very good example of living in the present, as I see things differently when I have a camera in my hand. It is also a good example of a Flow activity (see Chapter 2). This is part of my enjoying "The Quality of Life Remaining".
4. **Exercise:** cardio and yoga. Most weekends I burn about 1,000 calories on my exercise bike and usually have two, hour-long yoga sessions per week. I love yoga; it keeps me flexible, trains me to enjoy the present, helps me focus mentally and even makes me enjoy my food more. When I started practising it, I noticed my blood pressure reduced. Because I enjoy it, I am able to find the time to have two sessions nearly every week.

Overall, then, I would say that I am broadly following my own advice – because I find it works. My portfolio of activities will continue to evolve and change. I do feel that, if I were to "stop" and not have any of this sort of activity to pursue, I would start to rot, physically and mentally, quite quickly.

I have, indeed, a lot to be grateful for, mainly, the support of my family, friends and colleagues and good health. Little has happened by accident – I have worked hard to create my opportunities. My clients often also tell me that the approach I have described in this book has worked for them.

I do hope you enjoy your journey.

Chapter 16

Thinking of Starting Your Own Business?

If you are considering your options for the next stage of your working life, maybe one of them is starting your own business. This is a radically different path (and that is why I have put it at the end of the book) but it may be one you consider seriously. If you are considering it, what are some of the issues you should think about? What are the lessons from some people who have actually done this?

I have worked with over fifty start-up businesses and am adviser, or non-executive director, to several early revenue businesses. I therefore have a good idea of some of the typical issues you might face in developing your own business.

Your motivation

One of the very first things to consider is your own motivation and how strong it is. Starting and developing your own business is likely to be between very and extremely challenging and may well need several years of little or no income, very hard work (there is probably no one else to do what needs to be done) and demand considerable strategic agility on your part in terms of what the business does. In every case you will need a very high degree of determination. It will almost certainly cost you a considerable amount in terms of foregone income – and may even be at the cost of close relationships. Most start-up businesses fail, and many entrepreneurs suffer from forms of burn-out.

In other words, starting your own business is not something you should consider if you are finding it difficult to obtain a more mainstream corporate job. If you wish to consider it at all, it should be because starting your own business is something you really, *really* want to do. If this is not the case, you should pursue alternative options such as a full-time job.

Do you have a viable idea?

The other set of issues to consider are around your business idea: what, dispassionately, is the evidence that your business idea could form the basis of a viable business? What is different and better about your idea from what is already being provided?

A useful concept here is the idea of a "Minimum Viable Product". The basic idea is to avoid spending a great deal of time or money on developing your idea but working out what is the minimum product or service that you can develop to the point of quickly testing it in the market so that you can get early feedback. You may well then need to quickly adapt your idea, or indeed, abandon it – a useful mantra is "fail fast". (On the other hand, many entrepreneurs succeed eventually because of unreasonably dogged determination.)

In any case, your business idea will have to solve a real problem and not just be a nice idea looking for a problem.

Finance

Unless you are starting a business as a specialist consultant in an area where you already have a considerable amount of expertise and contacts – as this would probably not require significant start-up capital – you will very likely need financial support for your new business, or at least be able to live with no income for several years. Certainly, if you are going to seek other potential investors, one of the first questions you will be asked will be: "How much money have you already invested in your business?" They will want to know if you have "skin in the game".

The most likely initial source of finance will be yourself and your friends and family. There are a few exceptions, but banks will be unlikely to loan you funds without an established and profitable trading record, and venture capital or private equity funds in the UK are only likely to consider investing if there is compelling evidence that you already have at the very least a potentially viable business – and preferably one that is already making a profit. (You may often feel with financing that banks and investors will provide you with funds – provided you don't really need them. A nice Catch-22).

Important questions

There are a host of other important issues or questions for you to consider:

- **What is the real purpose of your business?** Are you clear about what it is and are you highly motivated by it? Can you explain it in two sentences?
- **What support, including psychological support, will you have** from friends, family or business partners?
- **Are you ready to devote, say, three years, to the development of this business?** It very nearly always takes longer than you think to develop a sustainable business.
- **Do you have a clear business strategy so you are clear about what this business will do and what it will not do?** If you gain evidence from the market that there may be better opportunities to pursue a somewhat different strategy, are you ready to change the strategic direction of the business at speed?
- **Do you like and trust any potential business partners?** Is there evidence they will be successful as entrepreneurs without any form of corporate support?
- **Why should potential customers buy from you** rather than anyone else?
- Have you carefully considered a broad range of **identifiable risks** and how they can be mitigated?

- **Do you have all the necessary operational skills** to make this work?
- **Are you familiar with all the key regulatory or legal issues** you will have to manage?
- As the business hopefully grows **are you ready for proper forms of governance** that will be necessary to maintain support from external investors and the reduction in your degree of personal control that you will be likely to experience because it is no longer just your money?
- **Are you ready to continue to try and develop the business whilst at the same time trying to raise external investment,** both of which are very demanding and time-consuming activities?
- **What are your thoughts about potentially exiting from the business?** How much is it going to be worth once you are no longer involved?

A more detailed exploration of these questions is provided in the Entrepreneurs' Checklist on page 279.

Four real life examples of entrepreneurs

1. **Bob Quick – Global Secure Accreditation Ltd. – Are hotels secure?**

   Bob Quick had had a very successful thirty-two-year-long policing career and had been responsible for national counter terrorism operations and the protection of the Royal Family. In 2010 he started Bluelight Global Solutions Ltd. that has conducted investigations in over twenty countries, provided intelligence in support of security, specialist security training and helped develop the Safe City platform.

After a lightbulb moment he also established Global Secure Accreditation (GSA) in 2018–19, which provides independently verified evidence that a hotel is relatively secure after research suggested that 80% of businesses had modified itineraries due to health or security concerns and 72% of business travellers suggested that travel risks had increased in the previous year.

The business was developing very well until COVID-19 happened and business travel stopped virtually overnight.

Since then, GSA has very successfully worked as a public sector service integrator for the management of approximately 100 Covid quarantine hotels and directly helped more than 12,000 emergency evacuees during the evacuation of Afghanistan. This has provided a critical and attractive contract and so put GSA on a more financially sustainable basis with more than 300 employees being recruited in a matter of weeks. As this operation has now concluded this source of income ceased abruptly and GSA is currently exploring and exploiting other related opportunities.

Bob's personal lessons during this journey were:

- Resilience – nothing prepares you for how hard this is.

- Setbacks – False dawns (e.g. COVID-19).
- Kissing frogs – network, network, network!
- Be careful! Not everyone is trustworthy.
- Persistence – get up, dust down and keep going!
- No plan survives – adaptability is key.
- Have an idea! It might not be the right one – but pursuing it will help you find it (the flash of brilliance!)

2. **Craig Thomson – Turntide Transport Ltd. – vertically integrated electrification**

   "I stood at one of life's many crossroads, my options were: mainstream and wait in the queue with everyone else, wear out some shoe leather and network, go it alone and take the entrepreneur's route or any combination of the aforementioned. I did exactly that – ALL of it!"

   In 2018, with a vision to create a vertically integrated, powertrain electrification ecosystem solutions business, a friend and I drafted a business "buy and build" plan over a coffee. With a strategy worked out, we went to market to source our funding. With little interest in the magnitude sought, £50 million, our focus switched to the US securing over £100 million, ultimately backed by Bill Gates, Jeff Bezos, Robert Downey Jr. and BMW i-Ventures, we engaged with Californian firm Turntide Technologies to broker and acquire not one, but three businesses in the northeast of the UK, to create Turntide Transport, a wholly owned subsidiary of the US parent.

Busier than ever, we successfully completed business realignment, integration, created our collective go-to-market strategy, that, if applied effectively, would take the critical mass of three SMEs acquired and create a future-ready entity with a desirable enterprise value in a GB£ trillions, marketplace-ready, to list or sell within five years. But, as Mike Tyson famously said, "Everyone has a plan until they get punched in the mouth". Craig is now looking for his next venture with more lessons-learnt experience.

Craig's personal lessons were:

- **Self-realisation:** You don't lose if you get knocked down, you lose if you stay down.
- **Self-awareness needs self-honesty:** Have moral fibre, stand by and live by your own values, understand who you are, what you can do and how you want to be recognised.
- **Most growth processes follow closely Sigmoidal (S shaped) growth curves,** it's therefore important to continuously create, innovate and anticipate in order to endure through time.
- **Energy** is the only universal currency, one of its many forms must be transformed to get anything done. Technology cannot turn a good enterprise into a great one, nor by itself

prevent disaster. Indeed, thoughtless reliance on technology is a liability, not an asset. Yet, when used right, when linked to a simple, clear and coherent concept rooted in deep understanding, technology is an essential driver in accelerating forward momentum (Jim Collins)

- "It is not the strongest of the species that survives, not the most intelligent that survives, it is the one that is the most adaptable to change" (Charles Darwin)
- Dare greatly, employ empathy, don't just have relationships, create connections.

3. **Alexander Seyf – Autolomous Ltd. – Software solutions for advanced therapy manufacturers**

Alexander Seyf built on his experience as a businessman. consultant and successful entrepreneur in the founding and development of a software as a service company, Autolomous Ltd., working in the rapidly developing industry of cell and gene therapy and dealing with the challenges and opportunities of rapid growth, talent acquisition and entry into the large US market whilst at the same time raising initial and second round growth capital.

Alexander's personal lessons are:

- Have an impactful idea that you believe in whole-heartedly.

- Realise it with passion, persistence, resilience, and endurance.
- Build your team based on decency and integrity and not only competence.
- Rely on no one but be open to trust some: get smart people you trust around you.
- Make a lifetime opportunity of the unforeseen.
- Hugely celebrate the smallest victories.
- Trust, cherish and nurture the culture of your company.

4. **Vibhav Nuwal – REConnect Energy – India's largest renewable energy tech company**

   Vibhav is the co-founder of REConnect Energy – India's leading Tech/AI solution provider focused on Renewable Energy. He is passionate about building new ventures and about sustainability. He tells of the development of REConnect Energy as he experienced it and his recent move to the UK and his exploration of a portfolio of activities based there.

   Vibhav's personal lessons were:

   - Your business should bring clear value to clients – show to the client, in max. two sentences, how you will make money for him.
   - Be shameless.

- Work on your co-founder relationship – it is the toughest relationship in the world.
- Leave a lot of room for self-doubt.
- Run experiments all the time, but at the same time, be ready to take a leap of faith.
- Build a unique business from the first brick onwards.
- Have the courage to think long term.
- Know what not to do – and communicate that clearly.

Conclusions: What the real-life stories tell us

These real-life stories are from completely different sectors and very different individuals, but their founders have learnt strikingly similar lessons from their personal experience:

- Before you decide to embark on an entrepreneurial journey you will need to be confident you have extraordinary resilience and determination to develop your business successfully.
- Your first idea may well not be the one that you successfully develop; you will need to be strategically agile.
- Rely on no one but be open to trust some.

I would add a further lesson from being involved in many early revenue businesses: you will have to be capable of *ruthless prioritisation*. In addition to managing cash very carefully you will need to be able to be highly efficient in the use of your own time and constantly establishing very clear and limited priorities.

Starting your own business is therefore not for the faint-hearted. When I ask entrepreneurs how they would describe their personal experience they quite often say: "I have never worked so hard in my life, but I have never had so much fun."

Enjoy your entrepreneurial journey. I wish you every success!

Below is a more detailed entrepreneurs' checklist for you to consider if you are quite serious about this option.

An Entrepreneurs' Checklist

If you are considering becoming an entrepreneur, your planning could be anywhere from having an outline idea to a fully worked-up business plan with funds. This is intended to be a generic checklist to accompany your planning. Some of these questions will be very relevant to your particular business – and some less so.

You will need to consider answers to the questions below to be confident that you will have a reasonably sustainable business and to present confidently to potential investors. The more positive the answers, the more likely that you will have a profitable business, with increasing value to attract investors.

Think about these issues before trying to write a business plan.

Purpose

Are you clear about the purpose of your business enterprise? For example, is it:

a. To provide you with an interesting and challenging lifestyle while allowing a sufficient income for you (and your family)?

b. To provide a financially life-changing event in terms of acquiring capital?

c. To allow you to apply your business skills to an area of real personal interest, more as a paying hobby?

d. To pursue a business activity that will provide a service that you regard as being needed by the world, meaningful and consistent with your values, and which will have a sustainable economic value that will continue beyond your personal involvement?

Your answer will colour your attitude to personal financial risk. For example, if you hope to use the development of your business to hopefully acquire a serious amount of capital, you may have to consider taking a corresponding degree of risk. It is not possible to successfully start and grow your own business without taking a quite serious set of risks, some of which will be personal.

Support/motivation

If you are planning to become an entrepreneur, this would have significant implications for your partner and possibly your children. Have you thoroughly discussed your plans with your partner? Other questions are:

a. Are you mentally prepared and resilient enough to work with no team initially, few mentors and no support mechanisms?

b. Are you ready to work harder than you have probably worked in your life, and take some of the biggest financial risks you have ever taken?

c. Does your partner really understand, appreciate and support your business concept?

d. Have you discussed with your partner and are you broadly agreed on the possible impact on your financial and personal futures?

e. Are you broadly aligned in terms of risk appetite regarding your lifestyle, such as making sure you would be able to support your children financially to the end of their education?

f. Do you have a contingency plan if this idea does not work out? Other sources of potential income?

g. To what extent have you identified other individuals who can provide you with moral support and professional expertise and who share your vision for the business? Can they provide something other than money, e.g. useful contacts?

h. If you have mainly been in corporate roles previously, your corporate life may have included a considerable degree of intellectual challenge and complexity. You may be used to working on interesting and complicated problems with interesting people. There are many challenges involved in setting up a new business but being an entrepreneur is often lonely and usually very difficult. Many of the day-to-day tasks may be quite mundane (e.g. preparing your VAT return). How do you feel about that?

i. To what extent does the development of this business fit with where you (and your partner) want to be in five years' time in terms of work-life balance, personal and professional achievements, financial position, etc.? How is your partner likely to react to what may well be three or so years with little or no income? What might the impact on your children be?

Time

a. It seems to be a universal law of start-ups that they take longer to reach breakeven than planned and therefore involve higher costs in terms of foregone income or cash outlays, or both. Are you psychologically and financially resilient enough to cope with these challenges and delays?

b. Are you (and your partner) prepared for, typically, three years of no income to establish this business?

Strategy

a. Do you have a very clear strategy of what the business will do, what it won't do, what type of customers it will serve and what type of service it will provide?

b. Why do you believe your strategy will be successful? What evidence or feedback do you have?

c. Is your business materially different from similar competing businesses in a way that is attractive to customers? (This may become clearer if you can compete on aspects other than price.) Is this difference capable of being legally protected? Can you, and do you, wish to patent any key aspects of the business? How difficult/expensive would it be for a competitor to establish a similar business?

d. Is it possible to test your business concept on a small scale that will not entail serious risk of time or capital?

e. Are all the key players in the company or team aware of the overall strategy and bought into it? Do you have enough constructive challenge to the strategy to adapt it as necessary?

f. Do you have sufficient time and are you close enough to your market so that you can sensibly react to market changes?

Management

a. Do you like and really trust your potential business partners?What is the evidence to suggest that you as an entrepreneur, possibly with one or two key colleagues, will be able to create value through the business concept?

b. How complete are the key skills in the management/ shareholder team, e.g. sector knowledge and track record, negotiation, developing prospective sales contacts, previous successful entrepreneurial experience, effective financial control, fundraising, etc? Do you have, or have access to, other specialist expertise that may be necessary, e.g. logistics, web development, manufacturing, regulation, technology, employment law?

c. Is your team seriously committed to making the enterprise successful despite the difficulties that will arise? Do they have something important to lose, and to gain, if the enterprise is successful or otherwise? Do the members of the team have somewhat different objectives and appetite for risks? After frank discussions, can you reach consensus?

d. Have you worked out, and is there consensus, on issues such as:

   Who gets how much equity? Why? What are the criteria for determining this?

   - How would a non-performing partner be removed?
   - What is the long-term incentive plan?
   - Will there be two classes of shares, e.g. voting for founders, non-voting for incentives?
   - For those involved from almost inception, have you worked out from when, and how much, salaries will be paid, how much each person will put in as risk equity?
   - How will you balance the interests of possible investors and management on issues such as salaries? Investors are unlikely to appreciate seeing much of their investment disappearing

from the company by way of salaries before it is significantly profitable.

e. Have you thought about what it is that you really *need* to do as the founding entrepreneur? Are there activities that can sensibly be outsourced/ provided on a commercial basis to reduce the risk of you working as a "busy fool" and not being able to devote enough time to the strategic development of the business, i.e. working *on* the business, not just *in* the business?

f. How will you deal with issues of share dilution? In successive funding rounds you may start off with 100% of the equity but end up with, say, 10%. On the other hand, it is more valuable to have 10% of a successful and growing enterprise than 100% of a small or stagnant business.

g. Is the key expertise capable of being passed on to professional managers after the original team exits? What is the business worth without you in it?

h. Do you have potential successor(s) to you in mind who could grow the business successfully after you withdraw, or do you just want to run it for cash?

Customers

a. Do you have a very clear idea of why a customer should buy from you as opposed to competing businesses?

b. What evidence is there that your business concept is solving an actual problem, as experienced by specific customers, rather than a solution looking for a problem?

c. Do you have evidence that the customer experience is a pleasant one and can you identify areas for improvement?

d. Do you know how many customers are repeat customers?

e. Do you know what your net promoter score is and how it is moving?

f. Do you understand your margins well enough to know which products/services should be expanded and which reduced?

g. Do you have reasonable bargaining power in dealing with major customers and suppliers?

h. Do the key managers in the business understand issues from a customer's perspective and are they in regular contact with customers?

Finance

a. Is the company structured appropriately to allow other investors to make tax-efficient investments, e.g. under the UK Enterprise Investment Scheme (EIS)?

b. Is the capital more than sufficient, e.g. more than twice as much as you think you need, for the first several years of trading, bearing in mind that unforeseen circumstances will arise, or things will just take a lot longer than you plan for?

c. In addition to first sources of finance such as yourself, friends and family, have you considered crowdfunding as a possibility? Crowdfunding is getting more sophisticated but normally works best for businesses that are relatively easily understood and which are quite local.

d. Is the financial structure of the business such that it should enhance returns to shareholders while being prudent in terms of the ability to service debt?

e. Is the accounting and control good enough that you can produce accurate management accounts within two or three days of month-end and your forecasting capability such that you can reasonably reliably forecast cashflows three months ahead? (If not, you are running some risk of insolvency.) Do you have enough capital to run for at least a year without income?

f. How much cash are you burning per month? Can it be reduced until you have more evidence of viability?

g. Do you have adequate capital to deal with very rapid expansion on a prepared basis rather than go to investors when your need is urgent, which would be very expensive in equity terms?

h. Can you arrange terms of trade so that your working capital cycle is as near as possible to cash-positive in normal trading?

i. Are you taking proper professional advice on complex financial and tax issues?

Risks

a. Have you identified all the foreseeable management, commercial, financial, IT, operational, market, cost, supplier or reputational risks that may materialise in the next two years that would be serious enough to put your business under threat? Do you have an idea how you would avoid or deal with them? Is your financial position robust enough such that you could cope with risks that cannot easily be foreseen?

b. Is your customer base growing and reasonably diverse, i.e. do your top five customers represent less than 40% of turnover?

c. Do you have appropriate insurance in place to cover any risks that would have a materially damaging effect on the business, e.g. key person insurance?

Operations

a. Do you have all the key operational skills in place to reliably deliver excellent customer service at an acceptable cost?

b. Do you have the policies, systems and processes in place, capable of rapid change as appropriate?

c. Have you identified appropriate premises at an acceptable cost? Do you really need premises, or can you do most things virtually or on customers' premises?

d. Are your suppliers reliable and capable of expansion? Are you heavily dependent on one supplier? How could this dependency be reduced?

e. Is your supply chain and customer service operation under effective control?

f. Do you have a clear idea of all the critical operational issues that must be addressed in the next twelve months and the means to address them?

Regulation and legal

a. Are you broadly familiar with the critical legal or regulatory issues that are relevant to your company, e.g. employment law, health and safety, environmental legislation, financial regulation?

b. Are you taking professional advice on these issues?

c. How confident are you that your company is compliant with all relevant laws and regulations?

d. Are there any potentially reputational or legal issues that could become a significant threat? How can these best be managed?

e. Who is in your crisis management team? Are they prepared?

Governance/legal/partners

a. Has the company been established as a tax-efficient and reasonably transparent legal vehicle?

b. Are the company's Articles straightforward, flexible and consistent with the company's actual business policies and shareholder agreements?

c. Are the accounts reasonably up to date, with clean audits?

d. Partners:

- If you are considering partner/investors are mutual expectations clear and reasonable?
- Are the basic motivations between the different founders/partners reasonably aligned?
- Do you have a very high degree of personal confidence and trust in your potential partners?
- Do you like spending time with them?
- How well do you know your partners in terms of integrity, competence, what they would be like to work with and the value they would bring to the business?
- Is it clearly agreed how much time and effort prospective partners will devote to the development of the business?
- Have you developed appropriate good leaver/bad leaver provisions in their contracts?

e. Do the main shareholders have sensible and well-considered shareholders' agreements in place that cover most likely eventualities, such as a desire from one partner to exit or from you to remove them, with terms that will not deter future investors? Are the agreements ones that reasonably balance the interests of the founding entrepreneurs and those who are investing in the business? Do the new investors have a reasonable degree of control or influence in the business to protect their investment but not so much that they risk de-motivating the founders?

f. Is there a board with agreed minutes of board meetings and at least one experienced director independent of the original entrepreneur so that founder's assumptions will be constructively challenged?

g. Do you have arrangements in place so that there are regular communications to all shareholders, and can they ask questions of the company?

h. Do your key employees have reasonable and clear contracts and terms? Are appropriate disciplinary processes in place such that you run a very low risk of a successful employment tribunal against you?

Fundraising

a. You are quite likely to have to raise additional capital in the first few years of your business. Are some of your friends and family likely to believe in your business enough to buy shares in it?

b. How will you value your business? (e.g. the price of similar businesses if you can find it, six times the profit in the third year of operation mathematically discounted for risk.)

c. Do you know angel investors who may be prepared to invest?

d. Can you prepare a compelling description of the business opportunity that is realistic as a one-page "teaser" document and a more detailed information memorandum? Will the statements in both stand up to a reasonable amount of scrutiny potential investors will follow in their due diligence?

e. Do you have a clear idea what you would spend investors' money on?

f. How quickly can you reach breakeven and how confident are you about this?

g. Do you think you will be able to both work on the development of the business and also spend time preparing investment documents, meeting with potential investors and answering questions? This combination is likely to be very demanding.

h. Will you be prepared to have a major investor as a director on your board and hence lose some degree of control of your business?

i. Are you prepared to have your shareholding significantly diluted by a major investment?

j. At what point should the business have an independent chairman of the board?

Financial difficulties

At some stage, especially in the first few years, it is quite possible that your business will get into financial difficulties. In these circumstances you will need to manage cashflow very carefully, rather than be very concerned about accounting profits. Key issues are:

a. Are directors confident that the company is in a position to meet its obligations, i.e. able to pay debts as they fall due?

b. Do you regularly update cashflow projection for, say, the next three months?

c. Is the company significantly exposed to exchange rate risk? Can this be reduced?

d. The overall circumstances of the company will need to be reviewed quite frequently and carefully so that directors can reasonably conclude they can legally continue to trade. (If directors continue to trade when they know the company cannot meet its financial obligations this is a criminal offence for which directors will be personally liable.)

e. If the company is in financial difficulties, you will have to carefully consider the interests of creditors more than shareholders.

f. If you are not sure what to do it is best to take professional advice from a licensed insolvency practitioner, who will be able to give the board good advice and avoid directors getting into a position where they may have personal or criminal liabilities.

g. You will have to communicate with shareholders and creditors carefully and give them a realistic view of the position of the company

Exit

a. Do you have an outline idea of how and approximately when you might exit from the business, e.g. trade sale, flotation on the Alternative Investment Market (AIM), or via a sale to a private equity house?

b. How would the business look today as a candidate for sale? Do you know the key issues that need to be addressed to ensure that a good sales value would be achieved and have a plan to address them?

c. If one or more of the founders leave, what value would actually remain in the business?

d. Will the founders/key executives be prepared to work on in the acquired company under an earn-out agreement for, say, two years after the deal so that the acquiring company makes sure it extracts the value from the vendors for the price it has paid for the company?

Setting up a Ltd. or Personal Services Ltd. Company

If you are providing any form of consultancy or forming a business for other purposes, you could probably do so as a sole trader (you just need to inform HMRC) or through a personal service limited company. If as a consultant you provide any advice on the basis of which people or organisations may act, and in particular, if there may be any perceived financial consequences that might flow from your advice, you should almost certainly set up a personal service limited company. You should write proposals, provide your services and invoice from that company as you would otherwise potentially have unlimited personal liability as a sole trader. In any consultancy proposal you should make it an express term of the agreement with your company's client that your company will provide advice in good faith and on the basis of the information you have been given but under no circumstances will you or your company accept any liability whatsoever for any perceived financial consequences of your advice. You may also wish to consider professional indemnity insurance. If you are working in a financial services area or with any organisation with a North American subsidiary, where the climate is often more litigious than the UK, you need to be particularly careful on the issue of your potential liability.

A limited company legal structure is generally simpler and more versatile than a limited liability partnership (LLP) where each partner's liabilities is limited to the amount they put into the business. LLPs are often used by accounting companies.

You should first think of a name for your company. I would suggest something fairly bland and versatile as no one is likely to give your company work because it has an attractive name. You can check name availability yourself via the Companies' House website and set it up either yourself or via your accountant. You can do this in a day or so.

The company will need its own bank account. It is usually easiest to start with your existing bank. Any bank will need to go through formal Know Your Customer processes and will ask you about the nature and purpose of the company, approximately how much turnover you expect in the first year and why you think that to be the case. This process can take up to six weeks.

You will need to keep good accounting records of all transactions and business expenses. Several software packages are available that may well be able to help you with this. If you expect to have turnover currently of above approximately £83,000 p.a. you will need to register for VAT, for which you will need to submit returns for on a quarterly basis. You will also need to submit annual returns and provide an annual profit and loss statement.

Your accountant will be able to do this provided you give them the appropriate information. In choosing your accountant it is important that they are used to working with small personal services or limited companies. You and any other director employed by your company will probably want to use your tax allowance and so you may well have to report PAYE on a monthly, or at least a quarterly, basis. It is your legal responsibility to ensure that there is always enough profit left in the company to pay corporation and other taxes and, although your accountant will help you, as a company director, you have final responsibility to ensure that the accounts represent a true and fair view of the financial state of the company.

The above process is exactly the same if you are setting up a limited company for any other business than consulting.

Further Reading

Cole, B. and Miller-Cole, B. (2017). *Self-Made: The Definitive Guide to Business Start-up Success*. London: John Murray Learning.

Mullins, J. (2006). *The New Business Road Test: What Entrepreneurs and Executives Should Do Before Writing a Business Plan*. Harlow: Financial Times, Prentice Hall.

Rees-Mogg, M. (2013). *Crowd Funding: How to Raise Money and Make Money in the Crowd*. New York, Crimson Publishing.

Bibliography with References

Anon. (18 February 2016). 'Giant sculpture moved after giving texters a sore head', *Salisbury Journal.*

Anon. (26 May 2020). 'Home sweet home: Almost three quarters of workers in financial services rate their working from home experience as positive', *Survey conducted by YouGov for Deloitte.*

Dusek, J., Outu H., Wohlhueter A., Bhasin, M., Zerbini, L., Joseph, M., Benson, H., Libermann, T., (2008). 'Genomic Counter-Stress Changes Induced by the Relaxation Response' , *PLOS ONE*, *12*(2) .

Burkeman, O., (2021). *Four Thousand Weeks: Time and How to Use It,* London: Penguin Random House. pp. 11, 31, 135.

Cooper, D. (2010). ''Career Planning – Mastering the Inner Game', Penna Senior Directors' Unit.

Danner, D., Snowdon, D., and Friesen, W., (2001).'Positive emotions in early life and longevity: Findings from the nun study', *Journal of Personality and Social Psychology, 80*(5), pp. 804–813.

Dolan, P., (2014). *Happiness by Design: Change What You Do, Not How You Think*. New York: Hudson Street Press.

ibid, p. 6.

Eichstaedt, J., Schwartz, H., Kern, M., Park, G., Labarthe, R., Merchant, R., Jha, S., Agrawal, M., Dziurznyski, L., Sap, M., Weeg, C., Larson, E., Ungar, L. and Seligman, M., (2015:). 'Psychological Language on Twitter Predicts County-Level Heart Disease Mortality', *Psychological Science*, *26*(2), pp. 159–169.

Felstead, A., Reuschke, D., (2021). 'A flash in the pan or a permanent change? The growth of homeworking during the pandemic and its effect on employee productivity in the UK', *Information Technology & People*, Vol. ahead-of-print No. ahead-of-print. https://doi.org/10.1108/ITP-11-2020-0758.

Forgeard, M.J.C. and Seligman, M.E.P., (2012). 'Seeing the glass half full: A review of the causes and consequences of optimism', *Pratiques Psychologiques*, *18*(2), pp. 107–120.

Gratton, L., Scott, A., (2016). *The 100-Year Life: Living and Working in an Age of Longevity*. London: Bloomsbury.

Great Britain. The Government Office for Science, (2008). *Foresight Mental Capital and Wellbeing Project*, Final Project report – Executive summary. London, p. 21.

Great Britain. The Government Property Agency, (2021). *Home Working and the UK Civil Service.*

Haidt, J., (2006).*The Happiness Hypothesis – Putting Ancient Wisdom and Philosophy to the Test of Modern Science*. London: Arrow, pp. 212, 138.

Hardman, T., Llewellyn, P. and Walker, S., (2021). 'Challenges of working from home during the COVID-19 pandemic', *Medical Writing*, 30(1).

Harter, J., Schmidt, F. and Keyes, C., (2003). 'Well-Being in the Workplace and Its Relationship to Business Outcomes: A Review of the Gallup Studies', *Flourishing: The Positive Person and the Good Life*, 2, pp. 205–224.

Ibaline, S. (2021). *The Stories of Immigrant Women Entrepreneurs in the United States of America*. Independently published.

Kellam, J., Kikuchi, L., Lewis, K., and Stronge, W., (2023). 'The Results are In: The UK Four-Day Week Pilot', *Autonomy Research*, pp. 6–7.

Lyubomirsky, S., (2008). *The How of Happiness: A Scientific Approach to Getting the Life You Want*. New York: Penguin. pp. 20, 22, 240, 244–245.

Mehrabian, A., Ferris, S. R. (1967). 'Inference of Attitudes From Nonverbal Communication in Two Channels', *Journal of Consulting Psychology, 31*(3), pp. 248–252.

Mehrabian, A., Wiener, M., (1967). 'Decoding of Inconsistent Communications', *Journal of Personality and Social Psychology*, 6(1), pp. 109–114.

Nettle, D., (2005). *Happiness: The Science Behind Your Smile*. Oxford: Oxford University Press. p.21.

Pryce-Jones, J., (2010). *Happiness at Work: Maximising Your Psychological Capital for Success*. New Jersey: Wiley–Blackwell. pp. 2, 6, 95, 100.

Quinones, E., (2006). *Link between income and happiness is mainly an illusion*, News at Princeton University, 4 August 2016. Princeton, NJ 08544.

Seligman, M., (2002). Authentic Happiness: Using the New Positive Psychology to Realize Your Potential for Lasting Fulfilment', *American Journal of Psychiatry,* 161 (45), (111), (936–937).

Smith, M. (2019). *Principles of Happiness.* Available at: https://youtu.be/WMD02R0rMCc.

Waldinger, R. and Schulz, M., (2023). *The Good Life and How to Live It: Lessons from the World's Longest Study on Happiness.* London: Penguin Random House.

ibid, p. 92–93.

[The] Yoga Biomedical Trust, London, (1983). Survey of (Self-reported) 2,700 who used yoga therapeutically.

About the Author

Mike Smith is a very experienced career coach and business mentor of executives. He has advised over three hundred executives over a broad range of sectors and nationalities. He has a particular interest in well-being on which he is a TEDx speaker ("Principles of Happiness"). Mike has also advised over fifty start-up companies. He is chairman of OfficePOD Ltd., and a non-executive director of GSA, which helped over 12,000 refugees during the emergency evacuation of Afghanistan.

He has worked as Chairman, CEO and NED of listed, privately and private equity owned companies in the UK, France, New Zealand and Australia and was a main board director of Scottish Power Plc during and after its privatisation. He later worked for seven years as a company doctor.

His early career was spent in Indonesia with Voluntary Service Overseas, a training role in a Liquified Natural Gas joint venture, followed by the Ford Foundation, and then working on a World Bank Mission to address long term Indonesian environmental management issues. He returned to the UK to take an MBA at Manchester Business School after which he worked for THORN EMI in positions of increasing responsibility.

Mike is married with four grown up children and has an interest in architecture (having built his own house in New Zealand and Scotland) and photography (mikeasmith photos on Instagram).

www.mikesmithworkandwell-being.com